Peel Your Own Orange

It's your business!

Author

Brigitte T. Murphy, Dip, BA, MBA

The People-House Productions

Dublin, Ireland

Published by The People-House Productions, 2010
P.O. Box 11926, Dublin 4, Ireland
Email: people-house@hotmail.com

website: http://www.peel-your-own-orange.ie

© Brigitte Murphy, 2010
ISBN: 978-0-9567148-0-0
A CIP record for this title is available from the British Library.

Book layout and design by Liam Heffernan
Cover image by Adyna at http://www.sxc.hu/
Floral graphic by Robert Proksa at http://www.sxc.hu/

The People-House Productions embraces the essence
of social entrepreneurship in its publications.

Printed by Walsh Colour Print, Kerry, Ireland

Open up your mind to exploring new opportunities

I offer a special gratitude to all the people
whom I have met over the years

Those we meet either drive, pull or inspire us
to move forward to another phase in our lives
while some just come to visit!

I would like to pay special tribute to the founding director of
Stira Folding Attic Stairs Ltd,
the late Michael Burke, who died suddenly on 15th August 2010.

Note to the reader

The material contained in this book is set out in good faith for general guidance and motivation. Laws and regulations are complex and liable to change, and readers should check the current position with the relevant authorities before making personal or business arrangements. No liability can be accepted for the loss or expense incurred as a result of relying in particular circumstances on the information in this book.

Publisher's note

Every effort has been made to ensure that the information contained in this book is accurate at the time of going to press, and the publisher and author cannot accept responsibility for any errors or omissions, however caused.

I dedicate this book to my parents.

Acknowledgements

A special thank you to Liam Heffernan for offering his encouragement, expertise and time, which arrived at a critical stage, and as a result the book manuscript made it into print.

Also a big thank you to Tony Somers who despite still adjusting to his director-ship and new life in Paris, took the time to edit the book, as did my good friend Dublin-based Marlene Lyng, a multi-tasking journalist and art critic.

Also thank you to Marcus O'Doherty and Peadar Faherty for their critiques of specialist sections of the book, and to Conor Sweeney for his willing legal advice when occasions arose, to Mary Bleahene and Sumi Nadarajah for kindly taking my phone queries; and thank you to readers: Rory O' Flynn, Mary and Yvonne Buttle, Sandra Clarke, and Martin Murphy and Brendan Lyons who also gave critical feedback.

A special thank you to Terry Clune, the Ernst & Young Entrepreneur of the Year 2009 for writing the Foreword, and to the other successful Irish entrepreneurs for giving quotes for the book: Mary Ann O'Brien, Dylan Collins, Denis O'Brien, and Michael Burke.

I wish to mention my mother Johanna Murphy, and again, my sister Mary, who have always been supportive at important stages in my life; and my youngest brother David Andrew for sharing his intellect and dvds, and for encouraging my trip to Brazil in 2007 where I met wonderful people, particularly Joe, who was instrumental in changing how I viewed my life. This book is a result of that renewed energy, focus and wisdom.

I am grateful to everyone who helped to make this book happen!

Contents

Preface

Peel Your Own Orange: It's your business! asks you to stop, think, and assess what you are doing, and how you are doing it every day. It asks you to dream your future through goal setting, and to make room for hope, no matter what your current situation happens to be. This book offers information and insights, which in turn, will enable you to realise that you have more choices, and have the power to create more opportunities in your life.

The first part of the book probes you to find out what you want in life, and helps you to set goals and find business ideas, all of which aim to guide you to find your business feet. As you progress through the different sections, there is more discussion on practical ways to start, operate and promote a small business, particularly with low level finance. Business is just a term, so business can be moulded to meet your lifestyle needs, no matter what level of talent, trade, profession or specialisation you possess. While I refer to business throughout this book, it just means that you get paid for what you do when you manage your own work, in your own time. A selection of some bite-sized business terms are explained at the end of selected chapters under 'Bibi's choice'.

The concept behind *Peel Your Own Orange: It's your business!* is to prompt and assist you to develop a business through insights and knowledge, but ultimately it is your decision to pick and choose what is relevant to you and your situation. The book is inclusive of the needs of those of you working in the creative fields such as musicians, fiction writers and artists, who have so often been set apart from business thinking through training and education, as well as due to economic, social, and business policies and traditions.

Everybody possesses creativity to some degree or another, and it is an invaluable business aid. It makes the planning process easier as it enables one to visualise possible outcomes of planned actions or inaction. Many people need more flexibility, more stimulation and vibrancy in their work which is often not satisfied by an employer, and often not even by ourselves.

Peel Your Own Orange: It's your business! recognises business as being part of a person's life rather then separate from it. The book dispels much of the perceived mystery about what is required to start a business, and what type of person one has to be in order to become an entrepreneur. The reality is that no two people have the same experiences, skills, aptitudes, or way of conceiving or doing things, so there is no one rule that can possibly apply to everyone.

Anyone can be in business. It just takes a little courage and information to journey towards entrepreneurship. The aim of this book is to help you to find your business feet for that journey.

Peel Your Own Orange: It's your business! is divided into different parts, each providing information and insights into key areas of business and market operations. It is a practical guide, providing you with the basic steps for business start-up, management and development, which can be applied to a wide variety of business types. The over-arching objective is to enable you to set and achieve your work and lifestyle goals so that you can experience a greater sense of achievement, and success. Life should never become an endurance test, so the least you should aim for is to make it interesting.

If you are currently without a job, then perhaps now is the time to plan for a new phase in your life and make it happen. Many people have things that they wish to do or achieve in their life but lack the courage to try. *Peel Your Own Orange: It's your business!* was written to encourage and invite people who may feel stuck or dulled by life, to peel off the layers of history and routine in order to allow change and new decisions to revitalize their lives. It is about self-exploration and introducing you to basic business thinking, because business can be for anyone, and that includes you!

Never be afraid to try
but be afraid to die having never tried!

Most people have the ability to manage their time, money, skills, experience, aptitude and attitude. You do it everyday. These skills can be combined to successfully run a business. The majority of people have barriers to manoeuvre around or overcome in order to find that little bit of extra courage and confidence to move forward. However, the positive person – which is within us all - will always find a way! So say yes to exploring and awakening the entrepreneur within you, and begin taking steps to set and achieve your goals.

Foreword

He who deliberates fully before taking the next step,
will spend the rest of his life standing on one leg.
~ Ancient Chinese Proverb

It can be tricky deciding where to begin - be it writing a book, or starting a business. Sometimes you've just got to jump in and see what happens. My business started from my mum's kitchen table in 1996 - she helped with the phone calls, loaned the seed capital, and gave what's needed most when starting out in business – encouragement.

Ideas for a business can come from anywhere! For me, I had just returned to college from a summer job in Germany, where I had paid 70% income tax. Naturally I wasn't too happy that so much of my college socialising fund was going to support German reunification. So I flew to Germany to demand my tax money back. After my first meeting with tax officials, I was politely told that I was not entitled to a refund. I went to another tax office, where I was duly informed that I had actually underpaid tax, and owed them a few Deutschmarks more. I decided to quickly exit for the lift, when I met another tax official who noticed my Guinness sports bag. Realising that I was Irish, his face lit up, as he explained his love for cycling in West Cork. He introduced himself as the Chief Inspector of Taxes, and asked if I needed any help, whereby he explained how I could successfully reclaim my German tax money.

Taxback.com has now grown to employ 670 staff in 22 countries, and become a leading global provider, helping people and companies worldwide to reclaim overcharged tax.

If I could give just one piece of advice, it would be to think positively all the time, searching for the good rather than highlighting the bad. A friend of mine refuses to use the word 'problems', instead he refers to 'challenges'. It's a subtle, but very effective method to change from how an obstacle is viewed. He was also highly involved with resolving the Northern Ireland Peace Process, and so knows a lot about differing views.

Imagine that feeling when you do succeed.
Think what it will feel like when you win.

Ireland is faced with significant challenges right now. But one major positive is that you are reading this book. You are looking for a solution. You are researching how to start a business. Ireland needs more people like you!

I met Brigitte Murphy, the author of *Peel Your Own Orange: It's your business!* while I was speaking with an MBA graduate group at the Waterford Institute of Technology. Sitting in the front row, Brigitte asked me so many smart questions that I thought she was either a journalist or a KGB agent! However when she later explained about the need for this book, I was honoured to write this forward.

The fact is that once your business starts, you will soon realise that bank debt, government instability, negative headlines etc will make no difference to you and your business, as despite it all - opportunity is everywhere. In all the chaos, it can be difficult to see, especially if you have lost during the recession. I started from home with mum as mentor, and on a shoestring budget, and had little need for banks as they would have refused me anyway.

To start with, you can do simple things – take a notebook, travel, and see new things, or see what others are not doing so well. Look outside of Ireland. If you speak English you've got a huge advantage. If a day begins badly, look to the positive-it will cost you nothing, and keep moving forward. The one simple decision which I made along the way which has been instrumental to our success is the decision to always be positive. Start each day with hope, and see the good in everything. Turn off negative news. Surround yourself with positive people. It's contagious. Especially when things are going wrong – look to the positive and look to the things you are good at, rather than the things you are not. Write down the goals you have for your business on yellow sticky labels, and put these on the fridge, beside your gearstick, in your wallet. Read them over, and over. Set rewards for attainment, and enjoy the reward when you achieve each milestone. At all stages you need to constantly innovate, do not sit on your laurels. Ask customers what you can do better. Ask your customers and staff for new ideas and areas for expansion.

> *Life is too short, so do what you love when choosing your business.*
> *In life, you regret the things you don't do - so just do it.*

I am a strong advocate for looking abroad for customers rather than at home. Our island population is limited – look globally, (like we do in Taxback.com). Success will be easier, and the rewards so much greater. We speak English, the language of business, we have connections globally, we are well liked as a nation, we have a unique system of government trade missions to help us promote abroad, and we are short flights from 3 of the 6 biggest global economies. At home, we have a beautifully green country, with lots of open space. We should teach communication and sales skills at national school.

Right now in Ireland, our country needs people brave enough to put their ideas into action, to make a start, and get their business started. More than ever in our history, we need more entrepreneurs. We are a global people. We have spread to every corner of the world, thanks in part to our past, partly to our education and our courage to move to find work and sometimes, a different way of life. And now we must use the global market place to create a future to be proud of, to get back on top! Learn to sell. Of course, things will not always go right, but it is how you react that counts. Learning from your mistakes, rather than quitting is the road to success.

Congratulations to Brigitte for writing this book, which helps to show that with a little knowledge and encouragement, starting a business can be for everyone!

I wish you success in your first and subsequent steps into entrepreneurship.

Terry Clune,
Managing Director, Taxback.com

Speaking from experience

Entrepreneur: Dylan Collins

Starting a company is one of the most challenging and fun things you'll ever do. It's an emotional rollercoaster where you'll go through incredible highs and lows before you've even had lunch. Even if it doesn't work out (and it doesn't always), you'll have learned more than you could possibly imagine and you'll be incredibly valuable whatever you do next.

Don't fear mistakes. They're the very best way to learn. If you're not making mistakes, then you're probably not making progress.

Always remember when starting companies that there are no rules as to what you should or shouldn't do. If and when you meet an obstacle, find a way of getting around it. People will always tell you why you can't do a particular thing but the very best thing is to just ignore it and find a way.

With technology, never be afraid to release something that's almost finished. Waiting for perfection can kill you, and if you're honest with your customers, you can go a long way with a beta tag :)

Dylan Collins, Jolt Online Gaming

PART 1

Preparation

- Introduction
- The 10-step guide to finding your business feet

Preparation

Introduction

Careful planning, research and flexibility can make the difference between success and failure, or contentment and stress. From childhood, you planned for things that you wanted to buy, places you wanted to go, the course you wanted to take, and the house you wanted to buy. Your overall life direction is no different – it needs careful planning!

You deserve to take time out now to plan, research, explore, and make decisions about your life and work. Perhaps being self-employed and running your own business is the option that you need to consider, and now is the time to begin on the path to finding your business feet.

The 10-step guide to finding your business feet

The thinking behind *Peel Your Own Orange: It's your business!* is that everyone should have the opportunity to grow the confidence to run their own business. The aim of this section is to get you to relax and explore the world in which you live, who you are, and to open your mind to allowing yourself to 'peel off the layers' so that you can see your abilities, skills and explore opportunities within and around you.

The 10-step guide

1. Creating your personal mission statement
2. Finding and setting your goals
3. Finding your business idea
4. Brainstorming for ideas
5. Researching your market place effectively
6. Timing
7. Start one or many
8. Location and business
9. Money
10. The benefits of a business plan

1. Creating your personal mission statement

Now is also a good time to begin to work out your personal mission state-ment, which will document the core values and the rules by which you live and wish to live. This will guide you in your decisions associated with all aspects of your life.

Developing a personal mission statement requires an investigation into both, what is important to you in your life, and your personal rules, and what you will and will not tolerate. It is fundamental to the kind of person you are, and may also greatly influence what kind of business you create, and how and with whom you will deal. As an example, my personal mission statement has for decades been:-

- to make a difference to others through what I write/produce
- to be independent – to have my own income and home
- to live my life with integrity, trust, love and gratitude
- to be mentally and physically fit and healthy

Although your character is fundamentally formed during childhood and early youth, some of your dearest values and aspirations may have sunk beyond recognition when you go to find your path in life. So they may need to be resurrected. It is only you who can recognize, recover, and present them for inclusion in your personal mission statement. If you are prevented from moving forward for reasons such as, lack of self-belief, or fear of success, I recommend, *You Can Do It*[1] by Louise L. Hay. The book, (plus CD), is relatively inexpensive and easily available. It was recommended to me by a friend, and I have found it an invaluable guide in overcoming these obstacles. There are times when most of us need reassurance that we are ok, and that we can, and deserve, to set and achieve more in our lives.

So begin to set yourself free of old ways of thinking. I recently came across a wonderful phrase: "Everyone is perfectly imperfect".[2] Perhaps it is difference which makes each of us perfect - perfect for the role that each of us has to play in the world. So embrace your life with confidence and self-assurance and believe that you are where you are meant to be right now! You must be, because you are, but you do not have to stay there!

---

1   Published by Hay House Publications, USA, 2004
2   Murphy, David Andrew, 2007

2. Finding and setting your goals

Your goals should be the guiding principles which drive the way you live your life, and earn your money. Action and your lifestyle choices are what you do in response to your expectations. So expect the best, and plan for what you want to achieve. Plan to achieve success. Work for it. Believe that it is yours. Recognizing what success means to you is part of the goal finding process. So start making your list which can take a lot of rewriting over days, weeks or months of thinking.

For example, if you wish to run a small business from home that earns you enough to pay your bills and include other modest activities such as holidays and socialising, then write that down. If you wish to make an impact in a literary, scientific or design field, then write that down. If your priority is to achieve high sales in a particular area, or to create a new product or service, then write that down. If you wish to be happily married and devote only half of your day to earning money through contracting out your skills, then write that down. If you wish to have a global online business, then write that down. If you wish to run an import-export business, then write that down.

Your goals are yours. They can be as ostentatious or conservative as you wish. Of course, your goals change as you progress through life. Therefore, it is important that you take the time to decide now what you passionately want to achieve. If your goal is a long-term one, then you should consider making a number of more readily achievable goals which you can reach en-route to your ultimate goal. It is with these long-term and interim goals in mind that you should begin your planning. Sometimes concentrating on one far away goal is exciting for a while, but enthusiasm can dim. By setting a series of interim goals you will stay on track more easily, enjoying smaller achievements as you move toward your ultimate goal.

3. Finding your business idea

You may not consider business as a possible option due to believing that you must find a 'new', or 'big and bright' idea. However, you do not necessarily have to find either!

Sometimes you recognize that you are not happy with your working life, or lifestyle. You know that you want your life to be different, but you do not know what to do next to change it! There are many books available to help you to try to find the answer, but perhaps you have to dig deep inside yourself and stop looking outside of yourself for answers. You could spend your whole life reading books, reviewing case studies, being an active fan of other entrepreneurs, but now it is your turn to take control of your own work and life! It is for that reason that *Peel Your Own Orange: It's your business!* does not present details of successful entrepreneurs as it would take you outside of yourself. It is so easy to live outside of your own world, and allow the years to slip by. I have come to believe that if you spend most of your time focusing upon the business and/or career success of others, you continue to find excuses to remain stuck in your own life. You cannot begin to start to turn your work and expertise into a business unless your focus is engaged in that direction.

Remember, many entrepreneurs had to start from where you are now too. It is never too early, and it is never too late, and everyone just has to find their own business feet at their level, and in their own time. Now is your time to decide what you want in your life, and how you are going to achieve it. Factors influencing how quickly you will get into business depend on the type of business you want, whether you wish to work fulltime, part-time, or focus upon individual commissions or contracts; your own skills, expertise, and if further training is required; and how you plan to operate such as from your home, from a shared or subsidized office space, your own premises, and if you need staff, transport etc. I am an advocate of starting small, and would recommend this approach for those with limited finance, and subsequently to grow the business in stages. However, a lot also depends upon your own personality, your support systems, and whether you are a high or low risk person.

So now that you have decided upon your goals and the type of lifestyle that you want, do you have a business idea? Ideas come, and go, and may return over days, months, or even years after having originally conceived them, but even then, you may not be convinced of their potential to make money. So with or without an idea, I suggest that you move to the next phase, 'Brainstorming'.

4. Brainstorming for ideas

Set aside a folder or notepad especially for your business ideas. Perhaps make it a brightly coloured pad as bright colours are associated with stimulating creative thinking. Being stressed is not generally helpful to brainstorming, but sometimes being driven to find a solution to a perceived problem is the spark that generates the business idea! Accept and work with your own situation, as that is where you are right now. Perhaps you might like to use the mantra which I have pasted to my computer and a wall at home:-

> *Believe that you can*
> *and you will*

Brainstorming is the action of putting all sorts of ideas on the table for discussion and review. It is about taking down the walls of your normal thinking, and allowing innovation and creativity to become part of your thought generation process. It could be useful for you to organize a brainstorming session with a very small group of people, perhaps calling on trusted friends, industry colleagues or family or a mix of these. If relevant expertise lies within this group, you may wish to make them your business associates. While working alone gives you total autonomy, working with people can prove to be much more fulfilling, inspiring, and energising despite some frustrations which arise on occasions. Your ideas can be stolen but remember - nobody can do it in exactly the way that you will do it.

However, it is important to be smart. Brainstorming by nature should provoke random thoughts and analysis. It is about the mission - to find a viable business idea - not about personalities. Ultimately, you have to decide if the input from others would be a positive input into your way of working and living, or if it would prove distracting. In a brainstorming session with a group, it is best to assign someone to lead the discussion, and that someone can be you.

Your methodology should be as follows: define the task and the results you want to achieve. Analyse each suggestion to see where it is going, and can go, if anywhere. Then revise all the suggestions and prioritise them by obtaining the level of interest among the group for each suggestion. You will in the end make up your own mind, but follow the brainstorming process for now. Allocate a person to investigate aspects of each idea, also checking the internet and other business networks for other companies operating in the same or a similar business. Establish the results. If the brainstorming session is successful you will have found at least one lead for a potential business idea. The next stage is to research your chosen market place. Only then should you progress your idea into a feasibility study.

If it happens that no idea appeals to you, I suggest that you read this book, give yourself some time and space, and do the brainstorming process again later.

5. Researching your market place effectively

It is essential that you research the market place in which you intend to engage. You need to see what is being done, and what you can do differently, or if there is a niche in the market that you could fill. You need to begin to work towards clarity on what you want to achieve, and research whether there is a need or opportunity for you to offer a service or product for sale within that sector.

Know your competitors. Be aware if what you do, or want to do, can be copied easily. Be aware and try to raise the barriers to entry for your competitors by making it difficult for others to copy what you do, and how you do it. This research, combined with brainstorming, must be repeated over, and over, until you are happy with the conclusions and analysis of the opportunities. This can be a slow process taking months or years, depending upon the complication of the business set up, as it can involve product research and development, and securing funding and/or investors. For many, turning a passion, or interest, into a business would be a dream come true, whether it is developing software programmes, being able to surf, bake, offer holistic healing services, write music, develop new designer labels, design new building structure concepts, and so on. However, some sectors/industries carry a lot of what is commonly referred to as 'red tape', and compliance is legally required, as breaches result in severe penalties. Government and industry regulations tend to be strict and normally offer little or no room for negotiation. So check out regulations and legislation before you make any moves to set up your chosen business.

If you wish to export and/or to locate your business in another country, then you would be best advised to set up a meeting with a representative from Enterprise Ireland and also the Industrial Development Authority (IDA). They have assisted many companies before you and will have a lot of information, experience and contacts to impart. Also connect with entrepreneurs who are already working in or exporting to that country, or countries as the case may be. Assuming that they are not threatened by your potential business start-up, most will be happy to share some of their experiences with you. Currency, legislation, culture, finance, and even the way of doing business may be different in that country. So be smart and research well, and do not be too proud to ask for advice.

6. Timing

There is no right or wrong time to start a business. Many say that a downturn in the economy is not a right time, but life does not stop because of that. It is important to note that sometimes there are increased incentives for enterprise development during and/or towards the tailing off of a downturn in economic activities. There is always the option to start small, start local and take your time building your business. Your local County & City Enterprise Board (CEB) should be a good source of information.

Perhaps you are considering baking cakes and tarts for the local shops. While you may consider that it may not require a huge capital investment, preparing food as a business will require that you conform to industry standards in health and safety which may incur unexpected costs in order to meet the established criteria for best practice. If you are contracting out your own skills as a business, for example, a lecturer or a designer, then your overheads and capital investment will be relatively low. However, keep in mind that money is always in short supply for the first-timer starting up a business. The upcoming Money section (no. 9) will show that the preparation you put into your business proposal, and your personal development, will play a major role in your success in securing funding.

7. Start one or many

A business colleague once commented that you may as well think big as it is as easy to open and manage many units as it is to open and manage just one. The rationale was that you would be giving the business all your time anyway, and if your units are using the same business model, then it would be relatively easy to manage. This would mean that time is shared across the many rather than spent obsessing about one business unit – you would feel just as tired with one as you would with many. It also suggests the possibility of getting rich quickly. However, if a multiple-business project requires you to invest heavily and it all goes pear-shaped, then you would need the courage to ride the storm. It would be for many reasons including the need for additional finance and/or strategic expertise that one could benefit from taking on a business partner or business angel, a move which could help to turn the business around through re-structuring. This could entail scaling-down the business and/or developing new business revenue streams and/or building new markets, because if you bale out, you could find yourself in a financial crater!

Being a low-risk person, I would err on the side of caution. I suggest that you do not invest big unless you know the industry well, have worked in it for years, have done your recent research, and can either afford to lose the money or find a way to repay it without losing your home or going to prison. However, you are the best judge!

8. Location and the business

Some people may wish to work from home and travel to their clients. Others will have clients visit their home. Remember to check that there are no residential/tenant legalities that prohibit you carrying on a business in your home. Some will set up a business that is web-based, liaising with clients, managing their relationships with suppliers, and operate a sales and marketing operation all from an office in their home, which could be the living room table!

Contracting out some aspects of your business is an option, but always try to get referrals for contractors. Create paper trails in email or printed form, as word-of-mouth will not support you well in the event of a conflict. If there is an aspect of business you do not like, or that burdens your time, then, if you can afford it, contract it out.

Remember that you can always invite a person to become a partner in your business that in turn brings its own expertise and a share of working capital. Terms and conditions should be clearly agreed and legally signed off. Working conditions should be as beneficial as possible to both parties. You do not necessarily have to work together daily. A lot depends upon your type of business, your lifestyle, and how you intend to manage your time and work. Once you have decided on the location, you then need to consider the business itself.

Also if you intend to employ staff be it full or part-time, health, safety and welfare regulations as well as employment, various registrations, taxation, and possible staff pension-related legislative requirements should also be researched to avoid any distress further down the road. Your local Revenue District (Tax) office or Enterprise Board (CEB), should be able to assist you with this information. Remember that every goal is achievable in some form or other.

So you will either have a business working from home or an office outside of the home. The benefit of good computer skills is an asset, and it is worthwhile investing in upgrading your own efficiency prior to starting your business. No matter what type of business you begin, you need to create a certain amount of operations - how and when you will perform tasks, such as online communications such as email and twitter, updating your website, doing online marketing, going into the market place, watching the activities of competitors in the market place, and online, phoning suppliers, contacting customers, doing direct marketing, sending out invoices, updating your accounts, submitting your VAT and your own and/or employer PRSI returns.

You will find your own style of business management as your business progresses, but a flexible attitude is best as there will be days when your schedule will need to give priority to demands of the office or the market place. You need to be watchful of market trends at home and abroad, and talk to your customers, suppliers and business associates. Becoming part of business networks will be helpful to you. Part of your preparation is to decide, not only who your clients are going to be, but whether you will serve the local, national, international communities, provide an online service and/or all of these, and what range of product or service you intend to provide.

You need to decide whether you are going to be *reactive* or *proactive* in business? *Reactive* means providing each client with whatever they require even if it is not within your expertise. This can-do-attitude demands a lot of time because you have to learn what is required by the client and to produce to order. *Proactive* means defining the range of services or products which your business is willing to provide, creating an area of expertise (broad or narrow), and operating within that remit. It is important to be mindful of what you want, and what your competition is doing and what is being offered into the market in which you work or wish to work. Perhaps you will implement a flexible approach, and access each job on request, and will accept requests if the remuneration is sufficiently rewarding or because you are glad to get the additional business. The state of your market place has a big influence on how you plan and implement your business operations.

9. Money

Not everyone actively seeks to be rich, just as not everyone wants to reach a high level of accomplishment or become recognized as an expert in their chosen field. However, all start-ups need money no matter what the ultimate goal happens to be. For most, the access to finance is challenging.

However, I have not given over any section in this book to the agencies which offer grants, and bursaries, as that is not what this book is about. It is about getting you to the point where you believe in yourself, have more knowledge and insights which enable you to find and formulate your business idea, and through your own skills and aptitude, will take it through to a viable business plan. There is a belief that once you get to this point, if your idea is viable, you will always find a way to make it happen. It is unhelpful for you now to focus your energy on obtaining grants etc before you find the power within yourself to take an idea to business plan and start-up stage. However, information on sources of finance will be provided at a later stage online on the website: http://www.peel-your-own-orange.ie

To start a business the most valuable element is the idea. Later comes concerns about funding. One advantage of the application for finanace process is that the feasibility of the proposed business is challenged at every turn, and you have to prove yourself capable and your business viable. All this preparation will make you an authority on your proposed business. The series of meetings with finance managers will in effect, give you free business advice. All this preparation will make you an authority on your proposed business. The series of meetings with finance managers will in effect, give you free business advice.

Many successful entrepreneurs start out with no money. Some stay in paid employment for as long as possible and then take part-time jobs to pay their bills during the start-up phase. Most start-ups take seed funding from family and friends. Many get support from national enterprise grants which are available at local/regional level on successful application. If you are thinking of export then the larger grant providers can be targeted and can look favourably on your idea, but normally one is required to be up and running before larger grant applications are considered. If you do an internet search for the country in which you wish to set up, you will find lots of information. All routes to finance should be considered open until proven otherwise, and even then, regard the response as temporary, as decisions are always up for review as policies change as well as decision-makers and market opportunities.

With regards to investors, some businesses bring in a business partner early on, while others wait until strategic development forces their hand.

It is wise to take time to skim through marketing and other business publications in order to remain informed of what is happening in the market place.

Most libraries will carry these publications and/or some relevant articles may be free to read online.

Take a break - review session

Having progressed through the 9 of the 10 fundamental steps to help you to find your business feet, you should now be in a position to answer most of the following questions. It is recommended that you answer these in writing, put your answers away in a drawer or electronic folder, and revisit them every few weeks and months to access if you are on target, or if you have deviated from your original thinking. Re-write what has changed, if anything. Performing this exercise helps you get greater clarity on your business idea. These questions will help you to assess your progress, prior to you formally sitting down to produce your business plan.

- What will your core business be?
- Do you have any/enough experience in this area?
- Where will you operate from?
- What do you want to achieve?
- What sales level do you need to achieve to break even?
- How will you structure your business?
- Will you work on a project-by-project basis or have a number running parallel?
- Will you work on commission/contract basis?
- Do you as the business owner want a private or public profile existence?
- Who are your target clients? (big businesses, small to medium-sized businesses, members of the public (householders, parents, students, etc), public bodies)
- How will you target your clients/get sales?
- How will you market your business?
- Will you focus on local, national or international markets?
- What are your short, medium and long-term goals?
- Are you highly motivated?
- Are you a positive person?
- Do you have a support network? (people you can turn to for advice/help)
- Are you willing to do direct selling?
- Are you willing and able to travel, if required?
- Can you afford to devote the time to start and develop your business?
- Can you sustain yourself financially while funding your start-up?

- Will you consider a business partner at any stage?
- Would you consider finding a sponsor to support some business activities?
- At what age do you want to retire?

If you can answer most of these questions, then well done! You are now many steps closer to achieving your personal, lifestyle and business goals. If you still do not have clarity on your business idea and cannot answer most of the questions, consider that it may be just a few areas in the business idea which are blocked, and not the whole idea. So do not panic. Talk it through with trusted friends and/or take time to visualise the idea or draw a flow chart of the process step by step. Do not rush it, perhaps relaxing and putting it into your subconscious (sleeping on it) for a few days or weeks may bring the solution. Maybe you will read again the idea-finding process. Remember, as a general rule, it is possible to negotiate in most situations so make a habit of talking to the key decision makers/owners. This can produce new ideas, new opportunities and/or save you money.

10. The benefits of a business plan

You have arrived at Step 10, the business plan stage, a time when you are required to sit, think and write. A business plan (as detailed in the next chapter) is the written document that becomes your road map to achieving your business goals. It is a key part of any business creation and development as it requires a detailed account of the whole proposed business operation with supporting research and documentation. It should be a flexible document and once it has been signed off by you, amendments should only be made when business, market or personal needs dictate change to benefit either you and/or the business. Also, as contract work (job by job or multi-jobbing) may become part of, or the sum of how you will operate your business, I suggest that you read the chapter on managing projects before setting out to write your business plan, as it may influence how you structure your business and document it.

PART 2

THE BUSINESS PLAN

- Introduction
- The nine key elements of a typical business plan
- Bibi's choice

Creating your business plan

Introduction

A business plan guides you to achieving your goals. Your goal is your destination. Your business plan is your satellite navigation (SatNav) journey planner. It will direct your route in response to you inputting the destination. It will automatically change the journey to facilitate deviations or mistakes that take the vehicle from the already planned road route. However, it is you who are the driver. In the same way, your business plan will need to be updated by you if changes are made along your journey or if you decide on a new destination. You are the brain power and source of information - a business plan is not an electronic device that can either read your mind and/or the market place so there are no automatic adjustments. Therefore, it is advisable to take regular breaks to review your progress, and the intended destination, to ensure that you are travelling on the route that will best meet your goals. The business plan is a blueprint for your business. It forces you to consider in detail how you are planning to achieve your goals, and how you will operate your business in the short and long-term. It helps you to refine your business idea.

Business plans have proven to be the best possible preparation for an entrepreneur because of the detail required in each section. It is also an important document representing the business when seeking partnerships, capital investments, or other financial facilities. Your business plan should be flexible. It is best if you prepare and save your document to your computer, as it enables adjustments to be made easily. However, do print out a hardcopy too, and file it for easy access, and remember that it is a confidential document. Into the future, it might be interesting to look back at your successes and challenges at the different stages of your business development, and to review the contribution that your business plans made to those achievements. Your success as an entrepreneur, may rise or fall, depending upon the preparation that you put into your business plan. It can save you time, money and frustration in the long and short-term. It should be viewed regularly, and amended only after due consideration. At different stages you may review the original goals in the plan and decide to make amendments, perhaps due to your own changed priorities, preferences, and/or due to economic, industry, market or other external factors. At other times, you might observe that you have deviated from what you had originally planned as your business map. In those instances, you must assess the profitability, opportunities, and benefits of the results of the detour. In the event of them being lower than what you had predicted in the original plan, and/or if it no longer feels comfortable, you may decide then that it is best to get back on track.

In the multiple-Oscar-winning movie, *Forrest Gump[1]*, the main character, Forrest, quotes his mother as always having said that *"Life was like a box of chocolates. You never know what you're gonna get"*.

She was right. Unexpected things happen. However, you still need to have a plan! You must have something to get you up in the morning, to energise you, to get you motoring, thinking and feeling in control of your life, and that something should make you feel good in yourself! It does not matter if you think that what happens to you is all fated, but it does matter if you drift and do nothing much to help yourself in your life, as you could achieve just that – nothing!! You learn nothing if you do nothing. Even if you fail at something it is a learning curve and another step forward. Sometimes you work hard and things do not seem to be working out, but then one day it all just begins to come together.

You will find examples of business plans on the internet. There are standard categories so it is up to you to pick and chose the categories that best reflect your planned business.

Below is a guide to the main parts of a standard business plan for any start-up company.

The nine key elements of a typical business plan

1. Title page
2. Table of contents
3. Executive summary
4. Description of the business
5. Marketing plan
6. Operational plan
7. Management and organisation
8. Financial analysis (including start-up expenses and capitalization)
9. Appendices (including supporting documentation)

---

1   Forrest Gump, 1994, Paramount Pictures, USA; Director: Robert Zemeckis; leading role: Tom Hanks; based on novel by: Winston Groom

1. Title page

This should contain the name, address, and contact details for the business. It should also contain the names and contact information for the owners, and as with all your documentation, the title page should be dated, and signed by the person who prepared the business plan.

2. Table of contents
(list of all the sections in your business plan)

3. The executive summary

The Executive Summary presents the professional overview of your business. This document should be clear, concise, lively and professional. It must inspire confidence in both you and your business. The Executive Summary is the first page to be read by people, such as, your bank manager when you are looking for a loan, and/or by a person wishing to invest in your business. Perhaps most importantly, the Executive Summary reflects your own plan for your product or service, your time, finance, and presents the overview of your business from start-up to the long-term vision. It is also a confidential document. I would suggest that you do not go around showing it to people unless they are going to be directly involved in your business. It can take you hours if not weeks to finalise this document which should be no more than two A4 pages. It should pull all aspects of your business together in a concise way, and should include the following:-

- the description of your business
- how you will leverage (use to maximum advantage) your product, service, and your skills
- who your clients will be
- in what type of market you wish to engage
- what national or international engagements you plan
- a profile of the owners of the business (you, and if you have a business partner/s) outlining what skills and experience they bring to the business
- what future plans you have for the business and how you see your chosen sector or sectors developing (nationally/internationally)
- how you will fund the business and the cash flow, for example, pay for goods, services, loan repayments, and so on.

Some suggest that the Executive Summary is best written after you have thought through and documented all the other aspects of the business. Personally, I suggest that you should write a draft first, then review and edit it after you have completed the first draft of your business plan or decide then if you need to start a completely new document. You will know instinctively what you need to do when that time comes.

4. The description of the business

Details about the business would include a detailed description of the following:-

i   Legal Structure
ii   Mission Statement
iii   Business Objectives
iv   Intellectual Property (IP)
v   Competitors
vi   Premises

i. The legal structure of the business
Define the legal structure of your business. For example, will it be a sole trader, a partnership, or a limited company as incorporated under the Companies Act? There are legal requirements for the setting up and operation of each of the above.
(For more on business formation options, see Part 7)

ii. The mission statement
This should be about two to three sentences detailing the reason for the existence of your company and your guiding principles. A principle reflects your values.
(For more on mission statement, see Bibi's choice, Part 2)

iii. Business objectives
Outline in this part of the business plan your core business activity; the distinctiveness of the products/services; state if it is a growth industry; discuss your business goals and objectives and how you intend to achieve your goals. State where you foresee your business in five and ten years time.

iv. Intellectual property (IP)

Outline if any intellectual property is part of the business. These are generally described as products of the mind, i.e. creative work, and include: inventions, designs, ideas, music, video or audio recordings, broadcasts, poems, journalistic works, architectural drawings, and maps. In this section you must include a list of any Intellectual Property Rights which you have obtained to protect your IP, such as patents, trade marks, copyright. Perhaps include a copy of the original documents in the Appendix.

(For more on intellectual property, see Part 7)

v. Competitors (include SWOT Analysis)

Mention your competitors and why and how you have advantages over them. State your strengths, weaknesses, obstacles and threats (SWOT) and outline how your weaknesses if any, can become strengths.

(For more on SWOT Analysis, see Part 6)

vi. Premises

State from what location you will work, how the business activities will be funded, and if there is a staging process involved over a number of years. For example, you may decide to begin working from home with the intention of renting/leasing a business unit or premises within a defined period of time. Outline the overhead costs, and how you will pay for them. State your ultimate aim, for example, to own your own premises, or lease several units, or create a franchise for your service, thus managing an administrative function from one office.

If it is part of your plan to have clients visiting your home office then state whether there are car parking spaces available or if you are located near public transport, as this could be a factor in a client deciding to do business with you or not.

The locality should be checked out to see if there are competitors nearby, if there are other complimentary service businesses that you or your clients can use, and if there is a banking service. However, with online banking nowadays, this is less of an important factor, depending upon your business needs. However, if you are doing e-business (online) then location is insignificant other than possibly being close to the warehouse or other backroom components of your business as you will need to visit to ensure that it is being managed to your satisfaction. If you manage it yourself then it has to be nearby to avoid wasting time travelling. You have to be practical and manage your time well. So set up with this in mind.

5. The marketing plan

Your marketing message and strategy will inform your targeted customers and clients of your existence and the services/products you sell and their benefits. Include in this part of the business plan a mention of any recent market research that you carried out yourself or commissioned from another source such as an agency. Also mention whether you will use a design company to produce your company image and logo (branding needs) and the costs involved, or if you intend to engage an Art and Design student to design for your business, and how you intend to reward them. If you plan a website then detail the costs, and at what stage in the development of the business that this will happen. If you plan to use corporate literature/stationery, then provide design and supplier details and outline the costs involved. State also the distribution method/s for business promotion.

Examples of marketing tools are, email formats, website links, flyers, word of mouth, trade shows, and offering interviews to local, national or global media. A business will use some or all of these at some time. However, it is smart to keep costs as low as possible, but remember that any investment in marketing is a waste of money if it does not achieve effectively your desired communication with your potential customers. So you must balance your spend with your objective.
(For more on marketing, see Part 6)

6. The operational plan

Outline in this section how your business will operate on a day to day basis. State details, such as staffing plans, including the number you wish to employ, their skill sets, job titles, the terms of engagement such as fulltime, part-time, seasonal, or just for the duration of a project. Mention the plans for outsourcing particular parts of the business or contracting specialists. List insurance details, any rental or lease agreements, (copies of these documents should be included in the appendix of the business plan), list necessary equipment, and the planned production and delivery process. Also outline your planned client relationship management policy, and the relevant functioning aspect of the website and any planned e-business. State if you plan to collect and retain customer information and if relevant, include a copy of your Privacy Policy for Data Protection in the Appendix.
(For more on privacy policy, see Part 5)

Security measures

Included in this operational plan should be an outline of what insurance measures have been put in place such as inventory control (if any products), and the system for maintaining financial and other records.

Quality control

Outline quality control measures and the system set up for customer feedback to ensure that your reputation for excellence in quality and professional services is maintained as it grows.

Customer service policy (CSP) document

In this section you outline how you plan to achieve best practice in dealing with your customers. For example, it states how goods returned are processed and customers are compensated and satisfied; it explains the complaints and follow-up procedure. It states the best practice in the ordering process, for example, the time duration within which an order is taken, processed and delivered to the customer. It outlines how in the event of a delay, the customer is notified immediately and given a new date of delivery. This new date should be acceptable and if not, is re-negotiated. The CSP mentions any loyalty card or other schemes operated by the company.

Stock management

The operational plan is complex. Stock management can be a core business activity, depending upon your business, and should be discussed at length to show your understanding of both business and consumer needs. So, if you are selling products, you also need to consider a Just-In-Time (JIT) stock ordering and delivery system. This endeavours to limit the amount of money unnecessarily tied up in stock for unnecessarily long lengths of time. It also works to ensure that where possible, no client is left waiting because you have run out of the ordered item. There needs to be an efficient ordering system so that the schedule is clear and there is no duplication of orders. Extra care must be used for the management of perishable goods and/or those with a limited lifespan. Customer satisfaction is the key to repeat business.

7. Management and organisation

Payment/credit policy document

This policy document must also be written to ensure that, as a new-to-the market business you do not give extended credit to customers due to your keenness to do business. Bad debts must be avoided if you are to survive in business! Debit card payments or cash are the norm for regular customers of business and fast moving consumer goods (FMCG). For services to clients, it is best practice to take a deposit at the booking stage and then request cash on the completion of the service.

When dealing with suppliers, they often allow 28 days credit. This can be in your favour. Perhaps you are a wholesaler, supplier, or contractor, and so you may operate a similar policy. However, if a customer does not pay within this time, no further services should be given until the account has been cleared. Prior to giving credit, it is good practice to check out new clients to make sure that they are not targeting new business as easy targets for credit for goods and services. You do not want a new client who travels like a honey bee from business to business leaving behind a trail of debts. Also state if you plan to use any type of online payment facility such as PayPal.

Customer feedback

It is crucial to get customer feedback. So whether this is obtained by email, over the phone or in person, a customer satisfaction form should be created at the early development phase of your business. In the case of service/contract work done, feedback should be secured on the day, or very shortly after the service is delivered. In the case of products sold, get feedback on the whole process from placing an order to delivery and satisfaction with your product(s).

Feedback from distributor/other agents

If you deal with distributors or other agents, it is good business practice to meet them in person regularly. Plan visits perhaps every few months to enquire about the processes and general operations, and to find out whether there is room for improvement or other services they would like from you. All this must be discussed in your business plan.

Operational duties of the owners of the business

The type of business formation you set up will define how you complete this section of the business plan, be it a sole trader, company, partnership or a trust. If you are the only one involved in the business as a sole trader, state your overall responsibilities for and to the business, and how you foresee that you can achieve these objectives. Outline your own experience and expertise that will benefit your business, mention the duration of your intended working day, and how you will be diligent in continually surveying your market place. Mention any access to expert advice within your family, industry, and/or

friendship circles. If you are a company, list the directors; and if a partnership list the partners; and if a trust, list the trustees. In each case, state what each person brings to the business, their responsibilities and involvement.
(For more on business formation, see Part 7)

Strategic operations

This is the overview of how you see your business functioning and expanding into the future. It requires a vision for the future. For example, will you secure strategic partnerships or associations at home or abroad, do you plan in the short or long-term to outsource some services locally, nationally, or internationally? Will you be a global operator? Is there a franchise opportunity for your business? Creating and developing a business requires considerable strategic thinking and planning.

The economic environment can be positive or negative depending upon the type of business you plan to create and develop. Perhaps you will buy an already established business and take it in a different direction. Even economic downturns can produce opportunities. Do your market research. Talk to people in business, join entrepreneur/small business groups, and listen to debates and economic reviews. When armed with information and different view points, then pay careful attention to your own instincts, particularly if they have served you well in the past.

8. Financial planning

In this section of the business plan, state how you will fund your start-up, for example, personal savings, loans from family, friends and so on. State whether you are eligible for grant aid and, if so, the source of it. Outline your long and short-term capital investment to support future development plans.

Mention if you plan to bring in a business partner, business angel or utilise venture capital. (see Bibi's choice below for explanation). State how you will manage the finance, whether you plan on purchasing or have purchased an accounting software package, and who will input and manage the accounts function. Outline any historical and projected sales, prices and profit margins. Outline if supplier credit has been agreed and give details. State your business credit policy, if any for example, 28 days credit or cash on delivery (for products and/or on satisfactory completion of service).

9. Appendix

At the end of the business plan, attach any policy and official documentation to support claims made in the plan. For example, any property deeds, copies of leases and contracts, insurance policy documents, documentation of banking facilities secured, business formation documents, director/partnership contracts, list of assets available as collateral for a loan, market and industry research studies on your business sector, and copies of advertising material.

Bibi's choice

A selection of business terms explained

Mission Statement: Many businesses have a brief mission statement which explains why they are in business and outlines their guiding principles. Some include it in their business plan, on their corporate literature such as annual reports, information packs for clients, distributors, agents and also post it on their corporate websites.

Objective: An objective has been described as a measurable step achievable within a defined period of time; it is derived from stated aims, and is described as being undistorted by emotion.

Goal: A destination point, for example, to make your first million (net profit). You can have long-term goals and short-term goals. The best policy is to have both, all progressing you towards achieving your ultimate long-term goal.

Business Angel: This is a private investor who will inject money into a business for a defined and agreed period of time and withdraw it with a profit. Angels tend to be business experts and usually require an active role in managing your business in return for the use of their money. On occasions you may find an angel happy to invest and advise, but not become directly involved in your business operation.

Strategic Partner: Another company or person that gives your business something that you need, for example, technology expertise, access to foreign markets, a distribution system or even capital. In return they gain benefit/s from having you as a strategic partner. It can also be that you bring your different areas of expertise together in order to engage in a joint venture (a shared investment in a business project, for example a new product or service), sharing the resulting revenue and benefits.

Venture Capital Investment: Where an investor invests (normally cash) for a long-term period into a small to medium-sized business, in return for a high interest return on their investment and/or equity (shares in the business). High risk businesses tend to give high returns to the investors in order to encourage investment which funds the business – be it in start-up or development phase.

Factoring: This is when you sell your business debts to a debt-collecting agent. They in turn will pay you often between 50 to 90 per cent of the total debt, and they then take responsibility (and the risk) of getting the money from the client. In the case of a 30 day invoice the agent may charge you between 3 to 6 per-cent on the total amount.

Speaking from experience

Entrepreneur: Mary Ann O'Brien

You have to be really resilient and persistent but if you have a real passion, then you can't fail.

Have a brilliant team behind you, and most importantly, get a good mentor who has experience and knowledge to share.

I think attitude and persistence count for a great deal. When I say persistence I mean dogged persistence, the sort that no matter what happens or what goes wrong you get up the next day with a can-do attitude knowing that an opportunity will present itself if you stay cool, calm and patient.

A more difficult challenge is when you find yourself flattened and de-motivated by very testing economic times that you work through knowing that everything happens for a reason, and in time you will look back and see what valuable lessons you learned through the problems you have to find solutions for. I think you will find you are a great deal smarter and stronger as a result.

Mary Ann O' Brien, Lily O'Brien's chocolates

PART 3

PROJECT AND JOB MANAGEMENT

Section 1

- Introduction

- The story of the local grocery store

- Project management – a business approach

- Managing your first project

- The project team

- The six main stages of a typical project

- The role of the project manager

- Working with committees

Section 2

- Budgeting - for projects and jobs

- Introduction

- Why budget

- Sample budget account plans

Project and job management

Section 1

Introduction

Perhaps in the past project management was seen as an exciting alternative to the general perception that business was a series of similar repetitive processes. In today's commercial world of ever-changing consumer trends, needs, and influences, of an economic, scientific and technological nature, business cannot afford to exist solely on the management of a series of repetitive processes. For many successful and progressive businesses today, business has become more akin to a series of projects being phased in and out on an ongoing basis. Every business is constantly evaluating where it is positioned, what it does, how it does it, what the competitors are doing. They are researching to find out if the consumer wants more, if competitors are offering more, and if their innovation is high relative to that of competitors, and are regularly assessing how more can be achieved. One must also track what is happening in other economic and trend-setting leader-countries and if the business is reflecting and/or working in the same direction. If not, then evaluate if that is either a good or bad thing and make adjustments if deemed in the best interest of the business.

The story of the local grocery store

The traditional small local grocery store in Ireland in many cases has been forced to close down due to lack of business. One contributing factor was that the owners (sole traders normally) did not respond to consumer needs. Perhaps they were unaccustomed to the processes of change. Change does not happen, it must be implemented, the scientific term is 'Effective Change Management' but that's another story for another time! The small grocery store did not innovate to reflect the changing times. They were, in a lot of cases across the country, replaced by more dynamic supermarket format franchise stores such as SPAR, Centra, and SuperValu. The typical new-style local 'grocery' stores now sell wine, provide a hot food counter, sandwich bars and/or salad counters, frozen and oven-ready food, sell lottery cards, provide in-store cash machines, and sell postage stamps. Many even host a Post Office service.

From a project management business perspective, one can break down the operations within the dynamic supermarket into different categories. Each category, for example, the hot food counter, probably started out as a special project when it was at its experimental stage. It progressed from inception where it went from idea into product trial, was tested on customer reaction in the store and/or other stores. Then based on customer reaction, and having researched what type of convenience foods are popular in other stores and what the consumers want, the product arrived at the ready to go stage. Following on from the successful completion of the special project it became a mini-business unit within the store.

Each mini-business unit brings in its own revenue steam into the business. Each unit now is managed for success, and new projects are constantly being sought, and put on a trial promotion in-store in order to ascertain market uptake. The successful/popular promotions are then costed, and if proven to be financially feasible (on an initial range from profitable to breaking even) they are developed to refresh and increase market share for the business. The added benefit is that it retains a competitive edge for the business (and brand) in the market place.

Project management – a business approach

A business may have a number of different projects running at the same time, or may run projects in parallel with a normal process-based product production line. Some businesses, particularly those involved in the consultancy and creative sectors work on a project-to-project basis.

The term 'project' is broad. For example, it can be a request to perform a task for someone, as it needs to be timed, priced, and all factors involved must be accounted for, such as materials used, travel costs, and so on. Some manufacturing companies will have new product teams working on a number of projects on an ongoing basis and they are under pressure to produce new products (or services). These in turn are launched under their generic brand names. This process of regular new product launches retains the brand buoyancy in the market place. It also allows the old products to be replaced by their new products which retains the excitement of 'new to market' and ensures that the revenue from the sale stays within the company. Just like a business plan, every aspect of any new product or service development is planned in advance of securing funding. Such plans include production details through to the involvement of public relations, advertising and promotion, transport and distribution.

Costs and time lines are allocated to every stage of the project including the approximate timing for the drawing down of the monies at each stage, and the expected delivery date and closing of that particular project.

Project management is essentially a process system. Every project is broken down into different stages across the period allocated, and interim reports are issued tracking the progress. A senior person is allocated responsibility for the project, and often a team of people is assigned or recruited specifically for the project.

Managing your first project

This is about you managing your project with confidence, being professional, and making sure that you make a profit (or at least break even) after all your costs have been deducted.

This chapter and the book as a whole should give you enough knowledge and insights to help you to introduce an effective operation and cost management system that suits your working needs. If you are taking a commission from another business or organization and your project is to create a particular work or perform a particular task, then you will be the person solely responsible for the success of that project. So guard your reputation. Read the project specification carefully and ask for clarification if you have doubts about any element of the project. You may need to bring in additional workers or specialists to assist you in parts of the work, depending on the job. Ensure that you cost your project before you decide to accept it. After all, you want to stay in business! You can agree in principle, but only confirm and sign when you have done your homework. Projects always have an agreed timeline – a start and a finish and/or delivery date. There is often a penalty for going over time. There may not be any extra funding available if you run over budget, so read the contract carefully.

Project management demands a detailed amount of planning and documentation, as normally you have to report to other people, be it the business or organization that commissioned you initially or the body funding your project work. Also if your business is built around commissions or different projects, then time management and budgeting is especially important. On occasions if you have a long timeline for a project, you may be able to accept shorter projects at the same time. However be mindful of how you manage your cash flow as well as your time. I suggest a policy of asking for a deposit of 50% in advance and/or agreed payments at different stages of the project. Therefore you can focus your attention on the work and timelines, and not be overly concerned about having sufficient finance to meet your project needs.

Learn to negotiate (a bargaining process). Always ask for a little more than what you require for a job, as that leaves some room for the bargaining process, and you the space to back down. This can leave the other party with the happy feeling that they have won the bargaining process and you with enough to cover your costs, and hopefully make a little profit. However, in a lot of cases a tendering process may exist and the cost becomes an integral part of the process in obtaining the commission. So do your costing homework well.

(For more on assessing costs/pricing, see Part 4).

I suggest that you set up a hard-copy project diary to ensure that you do not miss any key opportunities or deadlines, as you may not always be able to access the calendar on your computer. Computerised calendars are excellent in that they can be set up to email you reminders of key dates. It is possible to buy project management software for your computer which will assist your planning process. Enterprise Project Management (EPM) is a specified software system specifically developed for this. Make enquiries at your local computer store or go online if you have sufficient expertise to research the best software to meet your needs. Blogs can provide you with useful feedback and advice or if you are more comfortable talking to a person, then ask friends/colleagues and/or visit your local computer store for information on the most recent products. However, remember that you could always take the cheaper model which may not have the newest features, and would still perform the basic tasks that you need. Sometimes spending money is the easiest part of getting set up in business. So do not buy on the spot, take time to consider the purchase. Perhaps you should wait a while to see how you work, and then select the type of system that might best suit your skills and your own system of working, which in time will reveal itself.

The project team

A high investment project, costing for example, hundreds of thousands or millions, will most likely need all or some of the following people and areas of management expertise: project manager, project finance manager, research and development, manufacturing processes (depending on the project type/needs), marketing, sales and distribution and the core project team staff. An administration office would also be crucial for managing areas such as transaction tracking, payroll, taxation, and processing orders for the team and so on.

The six main stages of a typical project

For effective project management, a project should be divided into stages of development, and here is a guide to how to plan your new undertaking.

1. Understand the project environment

- Profile the target clients and consumers, for example define their age range, where they live, shop, went to college, their eating and entertainment habits etc.
- Define client/consumer expectations and needs and how they will be satisfied by the successful completion of your project as defined by you
- Define any constraints in trading with this category of customer, e.g. legal, taxation or other
- Outline the time, currency, cultural or political differences that can influence the project
- Outline the stakeholders of the project, their needs before, during and after the project
- Define how stakeholder needs will be satisfied on completion of the project

2. Define the project

There are five main components:-
i. Objectives
ii. Scope
iii. Strategy
iv. Success
v. Agreement

i. Objectives

Define and have clarity on the objectives of the project, state these in writing and be able to do a presentation for a client/stakeholder. The objectives must be both clear and measurable.

ii. Scope

To avoid confusion, delays or possible friction during the project, it is important to document the guidelines of the project before any final agreement is reached on the details. This is important from managing the contractor's expectations, and from the financial/commercial and legal aspects. The scope should be clearly documented as it establishes the boundaries within which the work will be performed, and this document can form the legal basis in the event of a dispute.

iii. Strategy

This defines how you are going to achieve the project objectives, which includes breaking the project down into time-based phases with each stage pin-pointed for review of progress and the project overall, and agree the details with the client. Comment: Story-boarding (pictorial representation of the stages of the project) is a good tool to ensure clarity on the stages of the project in your mind and that of each of your client/s.

iv. Success

Defining the success criteria for completion of the project is important for many reasons. Firstly, so that the project is correctly guided through the stages to the required end result; secondly, so that the reputation of all associated with the project remains positive; and finally, so that people get paid for the successful completion of their work. It is best if the success of the project is defined in terms of end-user satisfaction. This ensures that the reputation of your business is positively endorsed, repeat business will occur, and the product can be promoted.

v.   Agreement

If there are outside parties involved with the project, ensure that they all agree (in writing) on the terms of the project (particularly the objectives, scope, cost, and time factors) prior to the start date.

3. Project planning

Planning a project starts with defining the activities within the project. Define their cost and duration as well as that of the project as a whole. Define the level of resources required at different stages and overall. Define the timed stages and overall time plan for the project to ensure that it does not over-run. Ask questions if the project does not keep to the schedule. If necessary, allocate responsibility for the project to a project manager, and have that person agreed on by all the stakeholders if that is required. Define the project manager's responsibilities and communication duties in detail. By doing this, you ensure clarity should you find yourself off-track or should any queries arise as the project advances. The project must be broken down into achievable stages. Each stage must be detailed. These stages are normally referred to as 'gates'. Milestones should be set down at these gates along the project lifespan. On arrival at each defined gate the progress of the project will be reviewed to ensure that it is achieving its goals within the projected time and budget, and that the actual progress of the project is both measurable and sustainable.

4. Technical execution of the project

This entails putting production plans in place be it for a product or service. Establish technical/skilled expertise if and when required at the different stages of the development of the activities. Assign responsibilities to individuals within the project team. Define what is required of them. During the project, liaise with each team member to ensure they are performing as required and meeting the technical/skills requirements for the project, on time and within costs. Ensure that they are communicating with their colleagues when and where necessary.

5. Project control

Review and compare project progress with documented expectations. Communicate with team members for feedback. Review costs and any changes which may have occurred, such as supplier invoiced costs and overtime. Review any technical changes, delays in deliveries, problems within teams. Review and discover reasons for any missed deadlines in arriving at the 'gates' or for changes in standards or work schedules. Keep your finger on the pulse in the market place and note any changes that may impact upon the project, such as changes in technical standards that may affect the planned project, or competitors bringing similar offerings into your market, or emerging businesses that would benefit from being associated with the project.

6. Take the project to conclusion stage and to market

Ensure that the project momentum is not lost. Help to keep team players motivated to the end. Ensure the project is documented to the end. Ensure the follow-up document outlining the next stage - marketing and sales and distribution - is part of the final process which will promote the product/service in the target market.

(For more on marketing, see Part 6)

The role of the project manager

The project manager (PM) takes responsibility for planning, implementing and completing the project, beginning with getting the project up and running. If there is a team involved - part-time or fulltime - the PM is responsible for every aspect of their participation. The PM is responsible to the employer/the organization for the project itself and for the team members. I suggest that it is best if the PM is both a generalist and also has expertise in the type of project. Juggling must be done to meet all demands which can sometimes be conflicting. So the PM must have the initiative and courage, as well as the consultative skills to change the direction of the project or change any component of it, should s/he deem it in the best interest of the project and/or the organization.

Trade-offs can become part of the process of directing any goals within a project, and relate to time, costs and performance. It is when you are faced with these kinds of decisions that you need to have a clear vision in your mind and on paper of what you want to achieve, and where trade-offs can be allowed without lessening the success of the project. Keeping the project team concentrated and happy to the end is important to ensure that they stay to the completion of the project and do not abandon the team before it has been concluded. Perhaps offering some kind of incentive on completion should be considered to ensure that the project gets finished. Being interested in the team is important for the PM so that every individual feels respected for their input and reflects a positive outlook and positive energy for the team. Time spent communicating with the team is key, not just for the sake of the project, but also because you will be aware of what is happening in their lives, as personal life can sometimes impact upon the project.

Working with committees

Securing a project be it a commission or contracted job, can be made difficult when you have to deal with a committee, such as a board of directors, a project team, or an Arts board. So you must insist on one or two people from the committee being assigned to your project. If you do not, the reality is that you could end up with different people from the committee attending each project meeting leading to differing points of view and/or back-tracking on what was previously agreed, resulting in delays and confusion. So ensure that you get written sign-off on agreed project planning details prior to the start date and as you advance through each stage of the project. Document all meetings and send it by email to the relevant people. Copy all emails to yourself for your records. So whether you are a start-up business, or an individual who works on commissions/contracts, it is best practice for you to develop a policy where you agree everything in writing in advance of commitment to the project. You must endeavour to protect your business and your reputation.

Section 2

Budgeting – for projects and jobs

Introduction

A budget plan is a particular financial forecast (projection) and is normally done for a one-year period. Put another way, it shows the financial value of how you expect your business to do in different areas across a future period of time. Budgets are normally done for a wide range of areas where planning is paramount, such as: sales, stock requirements, cash requirements, marketing expenditure, new business presentations, costs (fixed and variable) and production costs. For large businesses, budgets can be organised to facilitate cross-company communication of information and assist co-ordination between departments. As a start-up, you will certainly need to prepare financial forecasts across all areas of your business in order to manage your time and focus on achieving your targets and goals.

Before you begin your business, one of the first budget plans must be a capital budget, which indicates your planned spending on longterm investment/expenditure capital items such as premises, office equipment, motor vehicle/s, and possible intellectual property licences such as trade marks, copyright, and patents. As a start-up it is easy to become excited and spend carelessly on capital using borrowed money. It is also easy to forget about the repayments which then become a big drain on your business cash flow. Intellectual property, particularly patents, can be expensive, and you might be better advised to find a partner who believes in the patent and will share some of the costs.

Why budget?

Based on researched information (historical/other), a budget plan will help you to get an overview of the financial needs of your business for the coming period, for example, it shows:-

- the quantity and cost of components or materials that you will need for your planned production or provision of services
- your expected cash receipts, in other words how much cash you expect to earn through sales or contract work across different times of the year

- the value and type of stock (raw materials) that you require to produce the products that you expect to sell or the services that you expect to provide
- the type and cost of your overheads and other projected expenses. Having this information to hand means that you can plan your financial needs to ensure that you will be able to meet your bills as they arrive. As we discussed before, we can use historical costs such as previous figures (if any) as a guide to future costs, but if you are new to business you will have to estimate your figures
- the busy times across the year when you may need to engage the services of one or more people. Budgeting for labour costs is important to ensure that you will be able to pay them.

Budgeting, like most aspects of business planning is not an exact science, but when the bills are due, you will have to come up with the money. So budgeting is well worth the time as it will save you many sleepless nights, and can be helpful if looking for finance to fund a project, or to fund a capital investment for your business, such as buying a new machine, software, automobile, or new premises. By being aware of your plans and objectives for the coming months/ year, it keeps your mind alert to new opportunities for your business. It keeps you motivated and on track to meet your targets. For example, producing a debtors budget will help you to track the amount owing to you, and will help to ensure that your credit policy is adhered to, and that clients do not extend their credit unknown to you as you need cash to meet your bills.

Budgeting is flexible and forward looking, and can be altered but as time goes into the production of a realistic plan, the budget should be adhered to as much as possible, as great job satisfaction comes with achieving goals. So give yourself something to celebrate!

However, very few people are highly motivated and happy everyday so do not give yourself a hard time if you have 'a bad day', because it's only that! Ideally financial statements such as the balance sheet, and profit and loss accounts, show sales and highlight many of the costs involved, and provide a clear indication of how the business is progressing. Most small businesses tend to produce the sales budget, and then produce a budgeted profit and loss, as well as budgeted overheads budget. The cash budget is important as it will allow you to plan and may drive you to change tactics to ensure that you will have the cash to meet all your needs for each month of the year. Producing a monthly overhead budget is a worthwhile undertaking for every small business, as having sufficient cash flow is one of the constant challenges.

As an entrepreneur you are the master of your own destiny. By producing budgets you are creating a system for monitoring, driving, and controlling the activities and challenges facing you and your business. Budgets demand research, and time to plan well, and it is generally done for a one-year period, broken down into months. It can also be broken down into two-month periods or seasons, depending on your business type and your need to assess your progress at different stages across the year. Budgeting for a year gives the company the chance to quantify its plans for achieving its objectives, and provides a yard-stick (or road map) against which actual progress can be compared in order to assess the business' performance at any given time along that year.

A year time-span is preferable for many reasons. For instance, it allows for busy and quiet periods to give an average result across the twelve months. It also allows for reaction to advertising or promotions, and allows the business the time to analyse and react to market and sector trends. It is also normal for a business to prepare long-term budgets (3-5 years), which reflect the goals of the business in terms of what it wants to achieve within that period.

Here are some simple samples of budget account plans for six-month periods:-

Budget Profit and Loss						
Month	**January**	**February**	**March**	**April**	**May**	**June**
Sales						
Cost of goods sold						
Salaries & Wages						
Electricity/Gas						
Depreciation						
Total Expenses						
Net Profit						

Cash Budget						
Month	**January**	**February**	**March**	**April**	**May**	**June**
Receipts						
Debtors						
Payments						
Creditors						
Salaries/Wages						
Electricity/Gas						
Other Overheads						
Loan Repayments						
Total Repayments						
Cash Surplus						
Cash Balance						

Debtors Budget (Record of monies due to you through credit sales)						
Month	**January**	**February**	**March**	**April**	**May**	**June**
Opening Balance						
Add Sales						
Less Cash Receipts						
Closing Balance						

Opening Balance: the amount currently owing to you in return for good/services sold
Receipts: people who paid within the month, usual term: 28 days
Sales in Debtors Budget: these are sales on credit

Creditors Budget						
Month	**January**	**February**	**March**	**April**	**May**	**June**
Opening Balance						
Add Purchases						
Less Cash Payments						
Closing Balance						

Stock Budget						
Month	**January**	**February**	**March**	**April**	**May**	**June**
Opening Balance						
Add Purchases						
Less Stock Used						
Closing Balance						

A master budget is an overview budget. It may incorporate a number of individual budgets. It would normally include: sales, production, manufacturing overhead, direct materials, direct labour, selling and administrative expenses, capital acquisitions, cash receipts and disbursements. It would also include a budgeted income statement, and budgeted balance sheet.

The following sample of a monthly management account and an annual operating budget may be helpful for contract/piece workers. It should be helpful in tracking the income and expenditure. It will also help in the costing of jobs as it is an easy-to-read document when you wish to do similar repeat jobs. This format can be personalised to suit any job or business requirement. These plans are best prepared in a spreadsheet document as extra lines and columns can easily be added or removed.

Jane Joslyn-Hill Sculpture Works Monthly Management Accounts Month Ended 31/Dec/2009						
Month / 2009				**Year to date / 2009**		
Actual £	Budget £	Variance £		Actual £	Budget £	Variance £
			INCOME			
			Grants			
			Other			
			Total			
			EXPENSES			
			Studio Rent			
			Light/Heat			
			Transport			
			Fees			
			Printing			
			Publicity			
			Stationary			
			Materials			
			Legal Fees			
			Other			
			Total			
			Net Profit/Loss			

Income less Expenditure = Net Profit (Loss).
Variance means difference (between the amount budgeted (expected) and the actual amount received).

A sample annual operating budget account

(prepare a column for each month, January to December).

	Jan	Feb	Mar	Apr	May	Jun .... Dec	
INCOME							
Grant Income							
Sales (Commissions)							
Other Income							
Total Income							
EXPENDITURE							
Studio Rent							
Studio Light & Heat							
Travel & Transport							
Entrance/Exhibition Fees							
Printing							
Publicity & Promotion							
Stationary							
Materials (pens, paint, paper)							
Materials (sand, clay, etc)							
Material (framing costs)							
Technology Costs							
Legal Fees							
Payment to Helper							
Total Expenditure							
Net Profit/Loss							

Note

Please do not expect to take in all the information in every section of this book in one read. It may take a few reads, and you may dip in and out of different sections. Remember, most professionals take years to study up on their chosen area, for example, marketing, business management, accounting, technology, and so on, so be patient, particularly if much of this is new to you.

PART 4

COSTING, PRICING AND GETTING PAID FOR PROJECTS AND JOBS

Costing, pricing and getting paid for projects and jobs

Introduction

This section deals with the main function at the heart of any successful business operation – costing, pricing, and getting paid for work done.

If you are new to the terminology, then read it a few times over a few days, perhaps each segment at a time. Perhaps discuss it with some friends as it can help to release any blocks to understanding.

Section 1

The critical roles of costing and pricing

Unless you recognize the existence of all the costs involved in your business, you may not be correctly pricing your product or service. This means that you may not bring in enough money through your sales and could find yourself with a cash flow problem, i.e. not enough money to pay your bills. Being able to recognize and charge for all your costs by including them in your pricing is a key function of effective business management. Sometimes costs such as overheads may be annual payments, so they can be spread across the year and an average cost per month is calculated.

Full cost is the term applied to the total amount of resources, usually measured in monetary terms, used to produce your product or service. For example, if the delivery of your product or service is part of what you provide to your customer, then your delivery costs should be incorporated into the overall cost of the production of your product or service. A profit margin should be charged, on top of your costs, in order to arrive at the sale price. The sell-at-any-cost mentality is short term thinking and if you persist with it, you will be out of business as soon as your cash reserves run dry.

Pricing is an important part of business planning. The price must be both strategic and practical. Your pricing model may change from time to time, depending upon many reasons such as whether you are doing a short-run promotion to encourage new customers, reducing price as a result of high volume sales, adjusting to reduce supplier or overhead costs, and/or setting your price to compete with the competition. The type of business that you are developing will dictate the type of costs that you have. Also increases or decreases in sales will impact upon costs and cashflow.

Section 2

Costing your projects and jobs

The main categories of costs are:-

i. Standard costs
ii. Fixed costs
iii. Variable costs

i. Standard costs
These are costs assigned to the average production of your product or service. This is the result of the addition of the different lines of costs such as delivery costs, wages, manufacturing overheads, cost of raw materials, and on the job application. Standard cost variance occurs when there is a difference between the actual costs incurred and the standard cost. This process of assessing the standard costs compared to the actual costs allows you to assess if your business can afford to repeat this project (product, service) and where savings can be made if any, or if you could do it differently. Managers are expected to control this variance by negotiation and manipulation of the prices and costs. However, changes in sales, inputs or distribution may alter the standard and more flexibility may be required, but costs and budgets must be closely scrutinized and managed.

ii. Fixed costs
These are costs that do not change when the business activity changes. Rent on the leased premises, leasing costs on machinery, and salaries, are examples of fixed costs. No matter whether your sales are high or low in any day or week, these overheads remain the same.

iii. Variable costs
As the term implies, these are costs that increase or decrease in relation to the increase or decrease in the business activity.

The grouping of similar cost strands will help you to more quickly manage, and assess the costs, and any changes in their production costs, be they products or services. Some other examples include the following:-

Indirect costs: These cannot be directly measured for each product or service. Examples are costs which apply to computer repairs, some phone charges, motor fuel bills, insurance cover, legal, and accounting services.

Direct costs: These are fixed costs that are directly related to the provision of the production of your product or service.

Allocated or common fixed costs: These are general costs and cannot be charged to a particular product line or service. For example if a number of services are provided from a particular office and by a set number of staff, then the office overheads (lighting, heating, loan repayment on computer equipment used by the staff) and the wages of those staff, are examples of common fixed costs.

Cost of sales: This is the grouping of all similar expenses incurred in the activities that produce and promote the product or service. For example, money spent on advertising, marketing or promotions, on the services of a sales person (or sales force), on the inputs (raw material, equipment, supplies) which enable the selling of your product or service. The delivery service, the cost of storage, and overheads such as lighting, heating, and business unit rental, are also part of your cost of producing your goods for sale. All these are costs which must be passed onto your customer when you are deciding on the prices/rates. When costs increase, you need to find a way to charge this to your customer which is normally through price increases or else it comes out of your profit margin.

Calculating direct labour hours: Time and motion studies suggest that a standard quantity of direct labour hours can be assumed for the performance of tasks/jobs. This is based upon the observation of work performed under simulated or actual working conditions and/or can be estimated from an analysis of past (historical) data.

Activity-based costing: This is where a business calculates a standard cost for specific overheads when producing a specific number of set ups, products or customer services to customers. For example, it will cost a business 2,000 euro to perform a standard graphic function for the homepage of a website for the average client. However, there may be variations depending on the customer needs, but this standard cost is based upon the amount of overheads including labour required to perform this service.

Incremental analysis: This is the assessment of the financial impact on the increase or decrease in your planned production of your product or service. For example, if an order is beyond your current capacity then you may decide to accept the order, and rent another premises, and contract some additional workers, so your expenses increase. However the increased production for a relatively small increase in cost, may overall reduce the cost per unit produced or service sold and therefore make you more profit.

Historical cost: A historical cost is a past figure (cost) which is used as a guide to project a future cost.

An opportunity cost: This is the value of benefits foregone by choosing one particular decision over another.

Project manage your costs

If you work on a project-by-project basis then you have to project manage your costs. For example, overheads should be spread over the amount used to produce each project over the particular billing periods. It can be a tedious process but is necessary so that you arrive at a pricing for your product or service that includes the costs involved in the production of the product or service.

For example, for a gas or electricity bill, calculate the percentage of time you used the gas or electricity (or both) for the production of your product/service. Get an average for the hours of the whole billing period and break it down into days. For instance, it took you 20 days to produce your design or complete the service. Divide your electricity (or gas) bill into days and hours. So you worked 10am until 10pm so that was 12 hours per day. 12 x 20 days = 240 hours. So charge the cost of electricity (gas) onto the customer for whom you produced the design or service. Another option would be to calculate the cost per day or hours across a year and then attribute that average cost to your clients' orders for goods or services. When there is an increase in gas or electricity, just increase the yearly average cost by that percentage increase.

If you work from home, you could perform a similar percentage calculation for the rent or mortgage. Typically this is paid on a monthly basis. So if it is a

30-day month, you divide your rent by your working days. So how much of that is for your work area? Is it used as your studio or do you live in part of it? If you live in part of it, then you should allocate part of your rent for personal expense and the other part to your business.

This brief case study in project managing your costs serves as a guide only. Each person has to work out how they wish to manage their time, their business, their money, and how they decide to split their costs across personal and business budgets. Perhaps when starting up, you may have to forego offsetting all the charges in this way until one has built up higher sales, in order to be able to spread the costs across a number of clients or products. To calculate costs per unit for a number of similar works produced, use the following basic formula:-

$$\frac{\text{the total number of unit works produced (direct+indirect costs)}}{\text{the number of unit works in the batch}}$$

Reduce costs - think sponsorship

Never get too excited when a bank grants you a loan. Nothing dulls innovation and saps energy more than stressing about how you are going to make your next repayment. While there are different types of loans and loan repayment arrangements and interest rates available, it is still money that has to be repaid when the date falls due. However, one way to reduce your costs and improve your prominence within the business and community sector is to consider finding a sponsorship when an appropriate opportunity arises.

(For more on sponsorship, see Part 6).

Section 3

Pricing your projects and jobs

Developing an effective pricing strategy is a challenge. So before we discuss pricing you need to decide on the following:-

- Is your product or service aimed at a specific type of user or buyer?
- Are similar products or services available in the market place?
- What is the price range available in the open market at present?
- Will people pay whatever price you set?
- What benefits will your business provide to your customers?
- If you have direct competitors, how is your service or product range different?
- Is your business a job by job operation?
- What is the profit margin that you wish to earn?
- What is the profit margin that you need to set so that you cover all your costs over a period such as six months?
- What are your fixed costs?
- What are your variable costs?
- Are you registered for Value Added Tax (VAT)?
- If yes, then you need to charge the correct rate of Value Added Tax (VAT) to your suppliers and customers for both goods and services. If you don't collect the relevant VAT from your customers and suppliers, it will have to be deducted from your profit margin when you make your VAT Returns. (For more on VAT, see Part 8)

Remember that as your business progresses it is important to review the systems in operation. Pricing strategies should be reviewed regularly, every week or even every day depending on your line of business. Competitors may have special offers or promotions or new services so you need to be aware of what is happening in your market place if you wish to stay in business and progress. You also need to keep a close watch on consumer and economic influences.

Some basic pricing format guides are explained in the following pages. The type of business you are developing will influence the type of pricing calculation that you decide to adopt.

Activity-based pricing

This is where your business offers its core products/se
additional charges for other add-on services such as packagıng
One example could be where the core prices vary according to the methou ..
to book an order, for example, in person, online or by phone. Another example
could be a hairdresser where there is an á la carte list of hair cut styles, colours
and treatment options, and your bill reflects what you have chosen. Activity-
based pricing can be expensive for customers, but they can also control how
much they wish to spend. Remember you are in business to stay in business
and need to make a profit. However, you should keep a close eye on prices -
your own and those of your competitors.

Target costing

Here you begin with the price of your product or service in mind which will produce
your target profit margin, for example a 30% mark-up on the cost of production or
your purchase price. This is a process where you produce your product or service to
meet the features of your design specification, after you have analysed your competitors' products and the customers' perceived needs and wants.

In large-scale operations, the ideal situation is when the marketing and cost
accounting staff are involved in the new product or service production phase
and the pricing includes all the costs. Too often the promotion and distribution
cost of the product or service is an after thought rather than being included in
the overall cost of production.

Cost-plus pricing

This is a simple-to-use system of pricing but its effectiveness depends upon
your business. It is where you put a mark-up on your cost price. You decide on
your mark-up, say 10%, 20% or 30%. The mark-up should allow for a reasonable profit and also needs to cover both your fixed and variable costs. Due to the
difficulty in estimating sales volumes and deducting a price according to that
volume of sales, many businesses use this cost-plus pricing model. However,
inherent in this pricing model is the circular process of economic theory, which
is that an increased price results in decreased demand, and the increased cost
per unit increases the price. This is deemed not to be a strategy for successful

- to attract people to your store, particularly if you are newly opened, or wish to get people new to the area accustomed to using your store
- to celebrate an event at your store, such as anniversaries

Section 4

How to pay and get paid

Remember that a sale is a legal contract. It is an exchange transaction between a buyer and a seller where a service or product is received in return for an agreed monetary value. You would be well advised to familiarise yourself with consumer rights and legislation before you begin your business. For example, sale and return policies can be a challenge for retailers, but everything can be managed once you are properly informed. Debit laser and credit cards are very useful for both buyers and sellers. However spending is easy and if you are a start-up business remember that it normally takes longer to make it than to spend it, so be mindful when you go shopping.

When paying online, the most popular and regularly accepted secure payment facility is provided by PayPal. As a start-up you should investigate how you can sell your product or service on your website. Check their website: http://www.paypal.co.uk

Using credit and debit cards, and giving bank and card account details on the website are the most common methods by which businesses and individuals pay for goods and services online.

If you use a debit card, payment is instantly taken from the card holder's account once the transaction has been approved. If you use a credit card, such as MasterCard or Visa, you have the option to pay the credit card company in a lump sum or by instalments. The credit transfer/bank giro option can be used to formally transfer money directly into another account and this can normally be done from most retail bank branches. You would need to know the person's bank, branch code and account number, and make sure that you spell their name correctly. A Western Union transfer is another option. The Western Union Company has agents worldwide providing consumer-to-consumer money transfers, and consumer-to-business transactions, and offers money order, money transfer, payment, and prepaid services.

ʹ ᴀᴌᴌ ιgh personal cheques are not used much anymore, if you do accept one, make sure that you get the payer's cheque card number written on the back of the cheque. A cheque card is only given to all creditworthy current account holders, and it is the same process for company cheques as for personal ones. If you do not have a personal cheque book, or do not wish to use one, then you can instead buy a bank draft or money order at any bank. This is a safe way of sending money through the post. If a cheque is crossed with, for example, Account (A/C) Payee Only written across it, then it cannot be cashed but must be lodged to the account of the person named on the cheque. Crossing a cheque makes it safe as if stolen it cannot be cashed over the counter as it is not transferable once it is crossed. Postal orders are money orders that can be purchased from Post Offices and tend to be used by people wishing to send smaller amounts of money through the post.

Travellers cheques are mainly used by people who are travelling abroad as they are a relatively secure method of carrying money. They can be cashed in the foreign country at the local rate of exchange. Receipts are given with the cheques so as that if they are lost or stolen they can be cancelled at a bank using the details on the receipt.

Euro cheques are blank cheques and can be written in foreign currency. When the cheque is lodged it will be converted into Euro and the money will then be taken from the account holder's bank account. It is necessary to also have the Euro cheque validation card, similar to a bank card for a cheque book, which is a cheque guarantee card. It is usually requested prior to accepting a Euro cheque as it shows that the bank regards you a creditworthy and reliable account holder.

A standing order is easy to set up, it is a regular payment from your bank account to another account. You can cancel it with the bank at any time. Repayments on short and medium term loans are usually paid in this way. The direct debit mandate is a similar option but is set up for the customer by the financial institution and cannot be cancelled without the agreement of the financial institution/organization to whom it is payable. A lot of club and social memberships operate this way also, giving them control over renewing memberships which fall due if the required notice is not received to discontinue membership in advance of the expiry date.

Charge cards are a newer phenomenon and are issued by a business to their regular customers, allowing them a money reserve that is based on the same principle as the credit card. A minimum must be paid off at the end of the month. The business must issue to the customer an account statement at the end of each month.

Bibi's choice

A selection of business terms explained

Just in Time (JIT): This is an operational standard which eliminates waste and enables maximum efficiency in the use of resources. It is a method of planning and control with the objective of meeting immediate demands for goods or services on time, with perfect quality and minimum to no waste.

Back-office: the behind-closed doors (low visibility) part of an operation.

Continuous Improvement: this is where the focus is on incremental improvements in operations across the organization, and is also embedded in an organizational attitude of always striving to do things better on a consistent and ongoing basis.

Core Functions: the functions that manage the main business processes of product/service development, operations and marketing.

Environmental Protection: a term given to the approach normally adopted by senior management and corporate policy to endeavour to minimize the negative impact of processes, products and services on the environment. Most developed countries have legislation in place to protect the environment and breaches of such legislation carry severe penalties.

Globalization: the whole world being part of the trading arena (supply chain).

Kaizen: the Japanese word for Continuous Improvement.

Lean: a management approach that seeks to eliminate waste at all levels of business operation.

Multi-skilling: increasing flexibility and motivation by increasing the skill sets of individuals enabling multi-tasking.

Speaking from experience

Entrepreneur: Michael Burke

People find inspiration for business from all sorts of experiences. I started out as a toolmaker having served an adult apprenticeship while in Australia and set up my own sub-contract engineering business in 1978. By 1982 we were tethering on the brink after two of our larger customers went belly-up. Then one day I was asked to repair an attic stairs by a friend who had moved back from America taking household contents with him including the attic stairs, I saw the problem and fixed it and thought 'Opportunity' because there was nothing else like it on the market. I started small, local, and grew.

Now, as a successful business owner, I can say that once you find the courage to take that first step, then all the next steps follow on from that. People find opportunities in different situations, you have to get on your path and see where it takes you, but have goals and plans and be flexible so when opportunities arise, you can run with them or not!

Michael Burke, Stira Folding Attic Stairs Ltd.

PART 5

BUILDING THE BUSINESS - Tools and Technology

Introduction

Section 1
Computer, email, and online facilities

Section 2
Websites and online selling

BiBi's choice

Building the business - tools and technology

Introduction

This section is intended as a basic guide to the benefits of technology for your business operation and development, while bearing in mind that some businesses will be technology-based and driven. It is not intended as an instruction guide to performing the different tasks. For this purpose, there are a wide range of books and guides available in both high street and online book stores, or to borrow from public libraries. This just gives you a flavour of some of the main benefits of the investment of your money and time in technology.

Many of you may feel adequately informed of your technology needs to support and develop your business start-up. Some of you may have never been exposed to technology in a hands-on capacity. So use this information as a stepping-stone to get you started. Even if you do not yet own a computer, with internet cafes widespread across most parts of the world, and internet access available in public and private venues from libraries to hotels, there is no reason for anyone not to use the internet for either research or sending emails. However, you should set up an email account to be used exclusively for your business.

Section 1

Computer, e-mail and online facilities - an overview of your technology needs

In this section, we take a look at some of the needs, options and benefits of technology for a start-up. Firstly, you will need to invest in a computer, preferably a laptop for its mobility. Secondly, you will also need to invest in a broadband facility which will enable you to link up to the internet in your own home/office, at other venues such as hotels, conference centres, and avail of the wire-free zones widely available in public places.

Services performed by your computer include telephone, email, online banking, operating computerised accounting packages, storing, manipulating and sending electronic pictures. Your computer will also store spreadsheets of data such as budgets and project information, contact names and you can also prepare and save PowerPoint presentation slides.

You can also use your computer for business, market and personal research and visiting websites. You can create your own website and upload information to it as required. Photographs can be uploaded to your computer directly from a mobile camera phone or from a scanner if using hard copy prints.

Circulating press releases, invitations and photographs by email is much more efficient than producing and sending hardcopies through the post. In business today, it is expected that you will have a website, just as you really need to have access to a computer to link into the global network.

You can also tune into many radio services online through your computer, and get regular news updates. Some television sites also provide on-demand footage of already broadcast programmes.

Technology in your business

The degree to which you rely and use your Information Technology (IT) depends on your type of business. It also depends upon how much you need to liaise with clients, potential clients and associates. In addition, your technology needs should be dictated by your longterm business objectives. It deserves careful planning so that all systems are compatible and can be integrated into your business operation either in the short or longterm. However, below are some immediate considerations:-

Security
With the increasing use of the internet, e-commerce, online banking, and mobile phones by government, public bodies, private and PLC businesses, and private individuals, and having regard to the growing proliferation of cyber crime, it is necessary and now also legally required that data-collecting organisations install systems to protect their computer systems and data. Reputations of businesses and professionals are also at risk of being seriously damaged if sensitive information is viewed or used without permission, stolen or lost. So, you should ensure that your computer comes with anti-virus and firewall security software.

There are different types of anti-virus software but in general it protects files and the computer memory against malicious software which can infiltrate a computer without the owner's consent. Firewall software screens for virus, and performs this task by filtering all traffic going between your computer and the internet. There are two types of firewall security systems – hardware and software – but ultimately, they both perform the same/similar protection functions at pre-computer access level. Firewall and anti-virus software security packages can be bought in stores, online or downloaded from the Internet, some free of charge, for example, AVG. Other brands include Norton, and McAfee.

Encryption is another type of security software that you will also need, as it will convert your plain text data files saved on your computer into a non-readable form. This ensures that your data and that of your clients' will be protected against unauthorised users, while it is both at rest, in transit, or if either your computer or portable storage device is lost or stolen. Microsoft Windows (XP, Vista, and Windows 7) comes with Encryption software.

An internet connection

An Internet connection is required to browse the internet (view website content), and to access email. Local providers such as, UPC, and Eircom in Ireland, provide these through a subscription system. Broadband has become the current established standard because of its speed. At the time of writing, entry-level broadband packages provide download speed of 1 megabit per second. This will support you browsing the web, online video viewing and the uploading of your own website.

File Transfer Protocol (FTP) is the internationally and industry-agreed method used to transfer files from your computer to the server sites/internet.

Your own website online

If you wish to create and upload a website it is required that you obtain the use of a server, as generally only large companies can afford or have the need to construct their own server infrastructure. Companies such as Blacknight Solutions, Hosting 365, and AOL provide this server service again on a subscription rate. It is best to get a recommendation before you decide on a hosting server service provider.

Why bother with the internet?

If you do not subscribe to receive the internet, you risk existing outside of mainstream communication, and missing out on key information.

For instance, you will not have the facility to send or receive emails, you will not be able to view websites and access a world of information at your fingertips. You will not have the facility to create and upload your own website and update it regularly and have other people visit it. You will not be able to sign up to receive newsletters which offer information and/or possible opportunities either directly or indirectly.

Sometimes by browsing the net you will get ideas, see what other people are doing and maybe get inspired to offer an online service yourself. 'The World is your Oyster' is an old adage, but the internet has made this a reality for personal, business and lifestyle choices and for all types of organizations today. Your world could be very isolated without access to the internet, because you would exist in an information black-spot. You would also exist without a major mass communication tool with which to make contact with the world - local, national and international.

Some 21st century internet-driven services

In addition, there are also other internet-driven opportunities and services which are a means of communication, interaction, and information exchange. For instance, YouTube, Facebook, chat rooms, blogging and twittering resources are available online. YouTube has become a strong communication tool to the extent that legislation is now active in some countries to prevent businesses and people from exploiting the review and opinion network which it has become. Also, it is now a trend for websites to host a link to their own footage on YouTube. As an indication of the popularity of YouTube, Sky News has a regular item showing the most visited YouTube sites. Twittering has also become a most popular means of fast email communication exchange used by members of the public at large, sometimes breaking news stories before the main media.

Podcasting is also a phenomenon for downloading data, for instance, music and radio programmes from websites. Mobile Apps are also a new emerging technology. They are mini-applications. They are particularly popular on smart-phones, such as the iPhone. Apps can be target-driven, for example, circulating them from a specific database to targeted or signed up individuals for the service, or made available on various platforms such as iTunes.

Much of the technology services mentioned above are available by subscriber service and/or are available free of charge. To become on online user, the first step is to sign up to an internet service provider, which in most countries, requires a fee per month payment.

By the end of the book, you will see how, at different times, some if not all of the above technologies can assist in some of your business operations, communication and information processes.

Buying a computer - software and facilities

While most people who own a computer believe that everyone else is knowledgeable about them, this is not necessarily the case. So if you are comfortable about your level of knowledge, you may wish to skip to the next section.

The cost of personal computers (PCs) and laptops have decreased greatly over the years, but for small start-ups, which may comprise of just yourself, the purchase of a computer can represent a considerable outlay. It is important to make the right choice, as it is an invaluable business tool.

If you are working in digital/graphic art, you may decide on an Apple Macintosh, usually referred to as an 'Apple Mac' by those familiar with the brand, as it seems to be the preferred model for those working in the graphics industry. No matter what your sector of expertise happens to be, you need to do your research before you buy, and this means asking questions of business colleagues and in the computer stores.

The main software system and facilities required by the average desktop/laptop computer users include: word processing; spreadsheets, databases, PowerPoint (presentation), Photo Editor, networking/wireless capabilities; a standard cd-rom/disk burner, USB ports (normally two) for USB keys (portable data storage units) and/or other connectivity use.

Most PCs come with a Microsoft Windows operating system. At the time of writing, the latest version of Windows is Windows 7. Some PCs may be supplied with earlier versions, for example, XP or Vista. So if you have Windows on your PC, it is important to check that any software you buy afterwards is compatible with that version of Windows. Other computer operating systems are Linux, Windows XP, and the Mac Operating System (Mac OS). For instance, the Microsoft Office software package is compatible with Microsoft Windows as it runs on the Microsoft computer operating system.

The Microsoft Office package comes with a range of applications such as Word (word processing) Excel (spreadsheets), Access (database), a PhotoEditor, and PowerPoint (presentation). While excellent, it is an expensive buy for the entrepreneur, who is usually working on a shoe-string budget. So an alternative software package worth considering is Open Office (from Oracle), which is available to download free from the internet.

Ensure that the seller knows all your needs and has the expertise to advise you particularly if you are unsure of the technical standards, facilities and accessories that you require. Also ensure that the files that you already have, be they stored on a CD, DVD, USB key (storage formats, not part of the computer) and/or are stored on a friend's computer, will be compatible with your new software. This will ensure that you do not encounter problems when you try to upload or edit between these files using your new system.

If you do not have access to broadband internet then you will need to buy a modem. The keyboard and mouse can be standard, and you can have the option to select the size of your screen, depending upon your supplier. The memory/storage capacity of your computer is crucial as it will determine the computer's speed and its ability to deal with pictures, website access and high volumes of data. If you buy a computer and find that it has an old version of software, know that it is probably upgradeable. If you find that you want greater memory capacity that too can be bought, but may require you taking the computer to the computer store.

Compliance

Compliance is the term applied to the process where a company, organization or individual seeks to ensure that all its activities, associations and registrations are operating within the law.

Apart from the obvious area such as health and safety, consumer law, and business law, there is software licensing (part of intellectual property law) which carries substantial fines for non-compliance.

An example of being in breach of a software licensing agreement would be, using a copy of a software programme that was purchased and used by someone else, and you use it but have not obtained the legal right to use it on your computer. To mitigate against this, always purchase your own software, or ultimately, use software that comes with a free licence.

In this book, I introduce the topic of compliance on occasions when it is particularly relevant to the topic being discussed. The reality is that the development of the European Union, increased international trade, communication and co-operation, and the growth of white collar and other international crime, has resulted in greater volumes of codes of practices, and legislation being introduced over the past number of decades. The fact that penalties are levied for non-compliance, one has to remain mindful and open to researching the existence and boundaries of the legislation at all times when starting up and operating a business. So if you are just starting out and are unsure about something, ask a professional for advice.

Training

A European Computer Driving Licence (ECDL) course gives an introduction to basic computer packages. It is an excellent foundation for gaining solid computer skills. It will give you confidence in operating your computer's various packages, enabling you to manage your business and your time more efficiently. ECDL courses are normally available in evening or daytime classes at local colleges, and are also available at more advanced levels.

Once your business gets up and running it will be much more challenging for you to relax and undertake a computer course and you will begrudge giving it the required time. So get that done as soon as you can. If you are reading this book and are still attending college, then do consider availing of all the possible computer training available while a student or in training, as in the market place courses cost money. If you are a practicing artist, then you might well consider contacting your local and national Arts organizations to see what courses they run and/or can recommend to you in order to further develop your technology skills. If you are unemployed/between contracts or just out of college, I suggest that you get on a course as soon as you can to up-skill or refresh your technology skills. If you are in employment learn all you can from your colleagues and take any possible training available to upgrade your skills.

Folders

Electronic folders can be created on your computer. This eliminates paper work and physical storage space needs and allows you to locate documents more easily. The setting up of electronic folders allows you to open a new folder for each new project so as you can access with ease all the data (pics, text, charts or diagrams etc) related to a specific project with one click on the relevant folder. So each of your projects has a single or many folders and can be neatly stored and opened when required.

The filing system on a computer is similar to the old office filing cabinet system. There was a cabinet, (now replaced by the computer), a drawer, (now a drive), and when you opened the drawer there were a line of suspended card folders (now you have a list of electronic folders when you click open the relevant drive), and when you opened the card folder with your hands, there were either one or many single documents inside, (now when you click open the electronic folder you have one or many electronic documents listed), or alternatively many sub-folders.

Backing up your data

A USB (Universal Serial Bus) is a portable electronic storage drive. It is some-times called 'a key' due most likely to the fact that once inserted into the rel-evant computer socket (port) it allows you access to the information stored on it. It is small enough to carry in your pocket or bag, as it is the size of an average adult finger.

You can save data (text, pics, charts, PowerPoint presentations, video etc.) to a USB key which is relatively cheap to buy. It is portable in that you can take the key to another computer system, for example, to a client's office and access your files there by just inputting the USB key into the appropriate port (socket) of the computer. Most modern laptops and desktop computers have a USB key port facility. However larger storage devices , eg. hard disk drives, are also available to buy which tend to have greater storage capacity, are more expensive, and are less easy to lose. Popular brands include Iomega, EDA and Western Digital, and 250 giga bytes should be an adequate size for basic office text, and data storage. A USB key can range around one or more giga bytes and is sufficient for backing up particular files but would not have the capacity to store whole office systems and/or drives.

However, if you need to visit a client's office and you are unsure about compat-ibility of your content with their computer operating system it is wise to check this out in advance. A phone call should suffice. If this is not possible, or you are not willing to take the chance (never a good option to 'risk it'), then take your laptop along or borrow one, having checked out its compatibility in advance, of course.

Backing up data is an advisable practice as if the computer crashes, gets stolen, or damaged, you will have a copy of your data stored. You can also store data on CDs and DVDs. However, there are computer service companies available whose business revolves around the retrieving of lost data. In a lot of cases, the retrieval of most of the information is successful, but it is not always 100% reliable. Data retrieval services cost money to perform this service, and during this time (normally a period of days) you will be without your computer. It would be cheaper and safer to buy the USB key or a hard disk drive to backup your files. The cost will depend upon the memory size of the drive that you need, but it is a cost that is getting cheaper all the time. So assess your storage needs. For instance, if you save lots of large pics, charts, or video footage, then you will need a large storage capacity. Staff at your local computer store should be able to advise you or go online.

Email

The concept of the email, and newer systems, such as Instant Messaging (IM) and AOL Instant Messenger (AIM) which are even more instant, have brought the global village into our lives on a daily basis as no matter where people live in the world they can be contacted directly once they have an email address, access to the internet, and are linked into their respective email account. To date email is still the most popular electronic communicating system in use. If you do not already have an email account, then it is time now for you to set one up.

Email accounts are available from most Internet Service Providers (ISPs) with a paid subscription. Free accounts are also available online, for example sites such as:-
Yahoo - http://www.mail.yahoo.com
Gmail - http://www.gmail.com
AOL   - http://www.aol.com
Microsoft Hotmail – http://www.hotmail.com

When selecting your email address, it is best to choose one that is easy to remember. For a business, the email address should contain your business name (if the name is available), or should in some way reflect the work that you do or intend to do. While you can play with the name, you may want to keep whatever you choose for many years so as that clients can revert to you or pass your email address to others. You need a relatively timeless email address.

When sending an email, additional files can be included, in a sort of 'piggy-back' facility. These are referred to as 'attachments'. To add the additional files, just click on the paperclip icon located on the email screen, and then search through the browse option to locate your file and click on it. These file attachments can range from word documents to photographs, video footage or audio files. An email can be sent to several people at the same time or just one person. This is how it saves the sender so much time by avoiding repetition. It is also a cheap means of communication compared to post, mobile phone, courier or personal delivery.

Electronic picture attachments are also far cheaper than having hardcopy prints produced in multiples, enveloped and sent by post. Instead the same digital picture can be circulated electronically to many people, and the quality of the picture stays the same. The receiver of the picture can also send it on (forward it) to others, also by email. Groups of email addresses can also be set up in your contacts folder under a title name. For example, under the title name Press, create a list of all the relevant newspaper editors-business, news, arts, health, and perhaps separate group listings for distributors, wholesalers, designers, clients, etc. This means that when you go to circulate your Press Release, invitation or information sheet, you do not have to key in each email address but can just click on the relevant group email address and your email will automatically send to each one listed in that group. Names can be added at any stage to any of the group lists.

Email etiquette in brief

The general rule is KISS - Keep it Short and Simple. Writing your emails in all capital letters can be interpreted as rude and aggressive, so best to use normal lower case with capitals in places as one would in normal hardcopy writing. Use a short and clear subject line. If there is a chance that your humour or phrase might be misunderstood, add a smiley symbol as cultural differences can create offence when none was intended. Be aware that smiley symbols may not always work if people are accessing their email on their 3G, blackberry or whatever type of mobile phone they have. It is best to be professional with professionals, so no slang, no abbreviations and always be respectful.

Email and internet on your mobile phone

If you have a 3G mobile phone, then you have the capacity for internet access. iPhone and other touch phones work with the most popular email systems which include Yahoo!, G-mail from Google, AOL, MobileMe from Apple, and the Microsoft Exchange email systems. Mobile email lets you send and receive photographs and graphics which are displayed in your message along with the text. Mobile email also allows you to view pdf, Microsoft Word, excel and other attachments on iPhone or other touch mobile phones. For instance, to set up your iPhone to receive and send email, the mobile phone operators have produced a user-friendly system where the user just clicks on the relevant icon on the phone's keypad to view the easy to follow instructions and options. If you need more information, you can put a question into a search engine such as Google and a list of website options to click on will be presented to you. Alternatively visit your local store or phone your local network support customer service line. Internet access by mobile phone can be expensive, so it could be smart to get quotes before you decide on a bundled-service (phone, internet and/or tv) provider. If you have the new Apple iPad computer, then you will also have all these facilities in one neat system. It comes with a built-in touch-screen keyboard or alternatively an external keyboard can be attached if required.

Create a contacts database

Collect people's names and contact details. Collect business cards. Keep records. This is your contact database. It can be invaluable when it comes to inviting guests to an event or researching sponsorship opportunities. In general, when you meet new people, retain their names in your files, as you may use their services or refer business to them, and maybe someday they may be able to do you a favour in return. However do not allow your emails to become regarded as SPAM, ie junk mail. So research your clients and make sure that your information to them is relevant and is not perceived as a nuisance. If you are holding sensitive client details then you are legally obliged to protect it, and encryption is the standard format. Always remember to backup your data, and to protect client contact information.

Pictures (pics)

It is best if you are sending pictures that you ask the receiver which is their preferred format, JPEG, PDF, GIF or another file extension. Pictures cannot be saved in the same format as some other data, such as text. Pictures require special software in order to retain their structure and detail. Some people may have a preferred extension format due to the computer operating system and/or the computer software they use.

You can upload a pic to your computer from your digital camera, the picture gallery of a mobile phone, a scanner attached to your computer or the scanner on a printer or someone else's computer which you can then email to yourself, open again and save to the appropriate file on your system, using the relevant extension. You can also upload pics to your website.

Remember at a basic legal level that copyright of the picture is yours if you originated the picture (illustration, photograph, etc.) and it is someone else's if it is not yours! In fact you can have a legal (copyright) message set up in your email account so as that it appears on all of your outgoing emails which is a good idea from both a protection and time perspective if you originate or represent yourself and/or clients who originate much of the material which you circulate by mail. This also applies to pictures, video, text etc. that you originate and post to your website.

Phone calls

Phone calls can also be made using your computer. It is particularly cheap for international calls if you use the Skype software available on the Skype website. If both people contacting each other have downloaded and activated Skype on their computers then your phone call is free. Skype is available in 28 languages and is used in almost every country around the world.

Also, some of the mobile phone companies offer discounts and cheaper rates online but this may vary. To make a call on the internet using your computer you will need a sound card, speakers and a microphone and the best time to buy these is when you are purchasing your computer. However, most modern systems have built-in sound cards as standard, but double-check before you buy. You will also need fast broadband with webcam when using video Skype.

Your online buddy 24/7!

Remember that if ever you need information on anything, go online. The Internet can be your buddy 24 hours a day. While you should not take everything you read as 100% fact, there is a lot of really good information on every conceivable topic. Always have information verified before you make any big decision with legal repercussions. It would also be expected of you to quote your source for copyright reasons. Remember not to download any information which might attract the internet security watchdog to your computer – such as pornographic files or special interest terrorist data – as the internet has a security provision built into it for the general welfare of people, business, politics and nations internationally.

Online networking

Do not use the internet as your only source of networking. Being self-employed can become relatively lonely, particularly if you are living alone. You need to meet real people and visit other businesses, trade shows, exhibitions, festivals and events, attend seminars where possible and become a member of business or special interest organizations, networks and clubs.

By all means work hard and smart at your business, but leave time for your personal side which can, on occasions, also bring you new business leads. A personal encounter is much more memorable than an email. A personal encounter has far more impact than a computer-based one, plus you can proffer your business card!

From a marketing and market research perspective, it is important to realise how big an impact social interacting online makes upon business and people both within and outside of the workplace. Certain categories of website are regarded as Social Networking sites. For instance, Facebook is just one such site and tends to be concerned with the personal; LinkedIn is also a networking site but is used for business/professional connections.

Section 2

Websites and online selling

Websites

Over the past decade the website has become a necessary part of business, as it facilitates online business operations. The first 'boom and bust' of that sector has come and gone, and it is still regarded as an integral part of most if not all business activities. For those who operate from home, developing an online business carries far fewer overheads than renting or leasing premises and requires fewer staffing and other associated services. Even if you had the premises you would still need a website as the majority of customers expect a business to have a website.

When it comes to buying online, trust is a factor. Operating a website is a key communication and business tool and needs constant monitoring and updating. People have come to learn that they need to be careful not to be too quick to input financial details without first checking out - the credibility of the sender in the case of an email received, and the credibility of the website if buying online.

The next consideration is marketing your website address. Just like having a nice home and wanting people to visit, you have to advise people of your address. Getting people to access your website saves on time explaining, for instance, what the business does, where it is located, and how it can be contacted. Your website is your own house of information. However, remember that visitors to your website will include your competitors.

The steps towards setting up a website should happen as follows:-

  i.   Register a domain name, ie a website address.
  ii. Set up a web hosting account
  iii. Design a website, which normally requires software, eg. Mozilla, or Dreamweaver
  iv. Test the website: ensure that different browsers view the content clearly and that content is configured correctly

v.   Using the web-hosting account, upload the website to the internet (using FTP) so that it goes online

vi. Run and maintain the 'live' website

Designing a website

Your website should reflect your business. Most importantly it must be informative, and also user-friendly. It is helpful to decide on a Customer Profile. Such details include the age range of your expected typical customer, their gender and lifestyle.

Your site must encourage repeat visits – it should impress them enough that they wish to tell their friends and business contacts about it. It is important that you visit other websites and decide which ones you like and why. Also consider the ones from which you have bought products or services and how you found the experience. Consider these characteristics and factors when you are designing your own website.

Designing a website can be done by you or by a web designer or you can do it together. Friends with web skills can be invaluable particularly if you cannot afford to engage a designer. However, ensure that you legally have full ownership of your website if you allow someone else to design it for you for free. A website should be regarded as an investment in your business development. Any problems with your website can lose you customers. If you have no experience in web design, then I would suggest that you collaborate with a website designer who can fill in the gaps in your thinking and skills to ensure that your website looks and operates in a user-friendly and professional manner, and reflects the look and feel of what you offer as a business professional.

To design your own website, you can start with the absolute basics ie learn HTML (Hyper Text Markup Language) and/or use HTML Editor[1] software to speed up the process. You can view a range of HTML Editors on the internet if you do a search.

Commercial website design tools are available to buy online and in stores, such as Adobe Dreamweaver and Microsoft Expression Web. There is also Sea Monkey Composer, which is a free alternative available online for you to down-

---

1   http://en.wikipedia.org/wiki/Comparison_of_HTML_editors

load. There are lots of website samples that can be downloaded free from the internet. To locate them, just enter 'free website designs' into a search engine such a Google and review the results. Google also offers a free website design download option.

Do internet searches and talk to user/s to find out which one would best suit your aptitude, interest and experience. There are also lots of books available on how to design your own website. You may have to review a few before you find the one that suits you. There is no one best route, but by having so much choice you will be able to find the best option to suit your needs.

You should engage the services of a professional web designer at different stages of building your website. Apart from the designing of the site, other complex elements include: installing the payment facility option, and uploading the website to the server. You have to sign up for these services and a monthly fee is normally charged. There is a growing amount of internet fraud today but the reality is that more and more people are buying and selling online. So, to encourage financial transactions online it is important that your website operates in a confidential and secure environment.

Tracking visitors to the website has become part of business analysis. A free online service facility provided by StatCounter.com[1], an Irish company, allows you to track the number of website visits. Being aware of the number and frequency of visits helps a business to assess any new marketing initiatives, as well as general interest in the site. Another more advanced, and also free service, is Google Analytics[2]. It will not only track the number of visitors to the site, but will profile and analyse them.

An effective website should include:-

- your core messages presented as the focus point
- a brief Mission Statement
- high presentation standards, for example, it should be easy to read and navigate by all/most web browsers
- your contact information must be clearly visible on the site
- if you are a company, your company registration number must be stated and be legible

---

1   http://www.statcounter.com
2   http://www.google.com/analytics

- your Privacy Policy, outlining your management of client information, is legally required to be available to read on the site
- a click-on option to sign up for product or service updates

Key word-links to your website

A search engine is any online search facility such as Google.com or Yahoo.com which allows you to enter an online search. The accuracy of the results listed is greatly influenced by the key words (word tags) built into your website structure.

The adding of key word links to your website is normal practice. It means that the site will be pulled up into the listing display pages once the domain name (website name) or any of the associated key words are put into an online search. For example, Forensic Frank Glass is a bronze sculptor. His art works are themed around mainly bronze eggs of all sizes and interpretations. So the key words he may have built into his website which will list his website if entered in an online search, could be: Frank, forensic, glass, sculptor, bronze sculptures, bronze eggs, eggs, bronze, artist, art, curves, kiln art. The list could also include unrelated words and names, such as Arts Council, Harrods of London, export, gifts, and this trend is growing.

Also, Search Engine Optimization (SEO), and Search Engine Marketing (SEM), as well as AdWords are based upon the same concept, ie use not only key words, but use phrases, text, etc. to secure a high place in search result listings. (For more on SEM, SEO, AdWords, see Part 6)

Privacy statement

Before you undertake the creation of this document, visit other websites to view their statements. Perhaps you will need to seek legal advice, but that decision depends upon the business you provide on your website. A privacy statement advises your website users that you respect their privacy and are committed to protecting the personal information that they provide. It informs them of the company or organization's privacy policies and practices, and explains how their information is collected and used. For instance, eBay collects personal data - for example, from web visitors, sellers and buyers - so it is perhaps a good example of a data collection and management website with a privacy statement worth viewing. You will find an example of their privacy statement on the eBay website, the link to the document is located at the end of the homepage, as is the case on most personal data management operating websites.

Legally protect your business

Perhaps before you go live with your website, you should read the section on intellectual property rights in this book (Part 7).

It is important to be aware of how these rights can apply to you, your products and your services. You should, for instance, register your logo as a trade mark, and perhaps your signature, and assess if there is text on your website that you wish to have copyrighted. These are some of the legal issues that you would need to check prior to going live with your website.

Insurance is a cost but also offers big protection and peace of mind. It is suggested later in this section that you take out insurance to protect products. In the Legal and Business section, it is also suggested that you take out third party insurance to protect both yourself, your property, your workers, and those who might visit your home/office to transact business. You should also consider taking out insurance against being sued for malpractice or negligence.

Professional Indemnity Insurance protects you against legal claims against your business for malpractice/negligence. It is compulsory for many professional businesses and services, such as consultants, accountants, financial advisers, architects, engineers, solicitors, etc. An online business is open to the same consumer, professional and legal scrutiny as an office-based business plus there is the additional duty of care required of any online business operation, much of which is discussed in this section.
(For more on indemnity insurance, see Part 7)

Going live

While you may have completed the design of your website, it will not be 'live' until it is connected to a server. The server takes your website into the public sphere by giving it a presence and listing on the internet. Unless you have access to a dedicated server - which most people and/or small businesses will not - you will need to register the name of your website, commonly referred to as your website address, technically and legally referred to as, the domain name.

However, you have to choose a name that is available - one that nobody else has secured as a website address. You will also be required to choose the extension for your website name, for example will you be a .com (worldwide), or a .ie (Ireland-based) or a .eu extension, which signifies the European Union. With the .ie domain tag your website can still be accessed from anywhere in the world.

When you enter your website (domain) name, (for example, ForensicMartin. ie) on the site of the domain registering agency that you choose (for example Register 365.ie) you will find out whether the name is available or not. Just keep going down through your personal list of name options until one is accepted. However, sometimes it happens that your name is not available with the .com extension, but is with the .ie extension. I would be wary of sharing a name that is only differentiated by the extension, even if the other business is totally different to yours, but that is ultimately your choice.

What to look for in a server (hosting) company

There are many server hosting companies available. A server company enables your website to go live to the online world. Do your research on your needs and the service that each company provides.

Consider not only the prices but also whether it is a 24-hour support service or, failing that, whether they operate within the hours that you expect the majority of your clients will be visiting or doing business on your website. You should try to get a referral from other similar businesses before you decide on one, as your service provider is instrumental to the effectiveness of your website and your online business as a whole.

Online shopping

Buying or selling online is still regarded in the industry sector as e-commerce. However, in today's high street market place it is commonly referred to as online shopping. Most websites provide selling opportunities for users to browse and buy. Some facilitate browsing and selling – these are typically auction websites such as eBay.

Operating a website comes with responsibilities. Depending on the product and the country, the registered owner of an e-business site must pay attention to matters of intellectual property rights legislation. Be aware of cyber (internet) crime, and ensure that you have as much protection in place as possible to protect yourself and your client details.

You must ensure that tax is paid if/when due and that the legal structure and the business product/service being offered are permitted globally.

Nowadays, the encryption of highly sensitive stored data is becoming more a priority due to computer hackers accessing information and the physical theft of laptops. Become familiar with the legal requirements for data protection and business conducted online before you set up your e-business.
For more information on this, visit the following website: -
http://www.dataprotection.ie/docs/Home/4.htm

Payment, online sales and compliance

To facilitate a sale, it is expected that your website is designed to accept a credit card payment. With this option, the payment can be validated and accepted instantly. Visit other websites to see how they operate their payment systems. In general, there are two basic components to an online credit card facility: a payment gateway and an internet merchant account. There are companies which can organize the payment option for you, offering a combination of the two components. One such example is PayPal's Website Payments Standard– which has proven to be one of the more secure server's to accept payments by either credit card or PayPal. Another similar service is provided by WorldPay. A bank may also be able to provide you with an internet merchant account. These have come to be among the accepted industry standards which are in constant state of upgrading and development. These transaction procedures are concerned with providing a secure environment in which your clients and customers can do business.

You need to be aware that the Payment Card Industry (PCI) Standards Council is a global, industry-led organization, which provides for the best practice in the management of the Payment Card Industry Data Security Standard (PCI DSS), PIN Transaction Security (PTS) requirements and the Payment Application

Data Security Standard (PA-DSS)[1]. In 2010 they issued their updated guidelines for compliance, and penalties can be levied (ultimately by the relevant card company) if breaches are discovered.

Once you obtain the data sensitive information, you are then required to protect it, as far as possible, from being accessed and/or abused by unauthorised sources, such as hackers and cyber criminals. This will involve obtaining security software for your computer.

Security software would require the installation of a firewall and anti-virus software to protect sensitive information, such as cardholder details; the encryption (encoding) of sensitive information such as cardholder transactions; and to show that the website has the capacity to have website traffic tracked and managed with a view to protecting its users.

Although an experienced designer should be accustomed to meeting these requirements, you must also be aware of your responsibilities if you wish to set up an online business.

Insurance

If you are shipping fragile or perishable goods, then you will need to research the issue of insurance to cover the cost of replacement. Some courier companies will do a deal on insurance and/or will have it included in their price under certain conditions. Some couriers have stringent guidelines on the packaging and labelling of items, and if you comply with these, then you may not require independent insurance to cover delivery. However, you might prefer to be more protected in situations where the value of the products is high and/or they are fragile.

Insurance is an important matter. You would need to decide whether the insurance premium is worth the cover that you would get in the event of a claim. Investigate public liability insurance, depending upon the nature of your business, your own travel and contact with people and also the events that you may organize or in which you will participate across the year. You could get an 'all-in' policy, or just take out ad-hoc policies as you need them. Remember, it is best to get a few quotes. Sales people always sound so friendly and helpful and be care-

---

1   http://www.pcisecuritystandards.org/index.shtml

ful not to say 'yes' to the first quote – even if you think for sure it is right, take the reference number, their phone number or email address. Talk to other insurance providers, compare information and talk to someone else in a similar business or a business-minded friend for their advice. In the end you have to make up your own mind as it is your business. When you are starting out, you need to keep your costs down, but you do not need to lie awake at night worrying over a matter that some research and common sense can sort out for you. Be practical, and do not skimp on necessary insurance, but be smart and shop around.

Pricing for online selling

Normally the tendency is for products and services to be available at a cheaper rate online, as they are operating with fewer overhead costs such as premises and administration. However, do consider the distribution (shipping, packaging etc) costs involved. For example, your cost to someone living in Australia might be different to someone living within the country of your business' warehouse or service supply source. Always check out what the other web-based competitors are offering and react by adjusting your price or hold your own ground, depending upon the exclusivity of what you are providing. Also if you have done a lot of expensive advertising, you must allocate some of that cost to the product and/or budget to regain it through the expected increase in sales across a given period of time. It is a good practice to review your price regularly as well as that of your competitors.
(For more on costing/pricing, see Part 4)

eBay

This is an American owned and managed shopping and auction website, which has been localised to operate in different countries. It has a global network of users. You might in fact consider using eBay to offer your products for sale at a fixed price or avail of their auction facility. It is simple and relatively inexpensive to use.

Registration to visit the site is free of charge, and if you decide to register as a seller, there is a low percentage charge which is relative to the value of the item that you have for sale. The eBay format is that you upload a digital photograph of the product you have for sale, with exact measurements and a written description. If you have many items on offer you can have many auctions simultaneously. eBay has millions of users who scan the site regularly so by registering to sell or auction on eBay you get immediate access to high volumes of browser-trade viewing.

Credibility is always an issue with any Online service. Offering email support is helpful in generating trust for any enquiries in relation to the item for sale. If you learn of the offering of a service or product in another country or globally which could complement your business at home or abroad, you might consider a strategic relationship with them. eBay offers a seller referral system, and is well recognised among buyers due to its established brand name. As part of their customer service, eBay also offers an appeals system. When it comes to business, the boundaries and success of your business are limited only by your own imagination!

Bibi's choice

A selection of business terms explained

Malware: An abbreviated term for malicious software. It refers broadly to any software designed to infiltrate a computer (or server or computer network), with intent to cause damage. The term malware would generally include the computer virus.

Blog, Blogger, Blogging: A blog is a website page where anyone can visit to make a comment. It is an online open journal available to internet users. The Blogger is the person who enters a comment, and Blogging is the process of doing it.

Blogosphere: This is the term given to the electronic space (medium) that facilitates the exchange of electronic communication between Bloggers; it is regarded as a platform on which individuals can voice their opinions. The messages can be read by internet users who are themselves non-bloggers. Bloggers are sometimes invited to events along with formal media professionals. Their influence on public opinion is growing to the extent that the Blogosphere is fast becoming regarded by organizations, as well as marketing and public relations professionals as a medium to be considered when organizing communication campaigns.

www: means the World Wide Web. It is part of the format for a website address.

Broadband: This is an advanced transmission connection system that carries multiple lanes of data traffic, travelling on different frequency bands. It facilitates high-speed internet operations. Today it is possible to get Wireless Broadband, wireless meaning wire-free (WiFi) within a predetermined zone, for example, a hotel, house, or office space. This facility is constantly being expanded. Mobile Broadband works on both fixed and mobile apparatus, so one can work anywhere with it. However, there are still some areas remaining within Ireland that cannot access the broadband facility which makes website and email connecting a slow to near impossible means of doing business.

WYSIWYG: This is the acroynm for What You See Is What You Get. It means that there are no hidden tricks or tools to know, ie what happens is the direct result of what you do.

Podcast: This is a digital file (audio) published to a website that can be downloaded to a digital recording device such as an iPod thus permitting listening at any time rather than having to access the website to do so.

'Cloud' Computing: Otherwise referred to as Utility Computing, it is not a new concept but remains a futuristic consideration for most businesses. It is where both software applications and data can be housed and accessed at an online site owned by, for example, Microsoft. So it will seem that the applications and data are being accessed from a virtual 'Cloud'. Businesses can sign up to this system by plugging into the online network rather than take responsibility for on-site software installations, updates, security, etc.

PART 6

SELLING • MARKETING • PUBLIC RELATIONS

Section 1
Selling
- Introduction
- Sales and selling – the key to success

Section 2
Marketing
- Introduction
- The complexity of marketing
- Online marketing
- Online media and communication tools
- Market segmentation
- Market research
- The fundamental principles of marketing
- Branding
- What markets should you target?
- Competitive advantage
- Why use a marketing agency?
- The benefits of marketing

Section 3
Public Relations
- Introduction
- The power of public relations
- How to manage in a crisis
- A SWOT analysis
- Sponsorship
- Be innovative

- Bibi's choice

Selling • Marketing • Public Relations

Section 1

Selling

Introduction

Before you start-up any business, you need to have some indication of your sales targets for your first three, six, nine and twelve months, as well as for the first and second years, and finally, an expectation of what they will be in five to ten years. No matter what business you intend to set up, it must be financially viable in the long-term. You need to be able to financially sustain the initial break-even period, or even a period when you sustain losses, until you are more well established.

If you are a a small business starting-up on a shoestring budget, you will do your own research. There will be no historical record (past sales) upon which to base your sales forecast. So you will analyse similar products or services in the market place. You will need to consider if and why your product will sell less or more. You will also need to look at your competitors' customer profiles and then analyse your own product (or service) and see how it compares. Decide where and how you will market your business range to customers, and the reaction you expect in terms of sales. The style of the marketing campaigns undertaken by your competitors and the design of their place of business (retail, online etc) is indicative of their targeted customer type.

It is generally a good idea to test your products or service in the market place before you decide to go ahead with it. You could run a trial period with a focus group, or do a promotion stand in a store, conference, exhibition, or wherever best you will find a customer base to suit your product or service, as this will help you to test your potential market and will give you some indication of the potential sales. The exception could be testing an intellectual property prior to having it patented or copyrighted, i.e. if that is your intention, and if it could easily be copied.

Sales and selling – the key to success

Unless you make sales you will quickly go out of business, as no sales means no money coming into your business. Sales are the core activity of the business, as no matter how nicely set up your business happens to be, you have to sell whatever it is you offer; be it a product, or your own skill as a consultant, or contractor, or whatever. So whether you are doing business from a retail outlet, a studio, an office in an enterprise centre, from home, and/or online, there is no point sitting around with your business cards and letterheads in a drawer, when you have potential customers that you could target. Sales are all about people. If you feel the need to do so, sign up for a sales training course. You are your own best judge of this decision.

Your sales message must be about providing a service or product that enhances people's wellbeing and benefits their life or business in some way, or that they can convert into opportunities for people, animals or things that they care about. Sales are about informing, stimulating interest, and persuading people to want and buy what you are offering.

Selling also integrates into your social, business and personal contacts directly and indirectly. It is best to enjoy the people aspect of your work, as it is often through people that you achieve a balanced lifestyle and remain mentally healthy while you continue to work hard to achieve your goals. However, sales are not confined to a particular medium in today's local, national and global market place. You need to use all that is available to you to market your goods and advise people of your product or service. You need to inform people when they can buy it, and from where, and why they should buy from you.

The trend is to advertise the price, as otherwise people may not make the necessary enquiries as they may fear or assume that they cannot afford it. Price can persuade people to make an instant decision to buy or not. Traditionally, the prices of luxury goods are not advertised as much as with the middle to lower range of goods and services. However, the impact of the recession of late 2008 saw a change, as the prices of many luxury items were slashed and the reductions openly advertised in order to induce sales. Sales promotions tend to be short-term in order to create a novelty factor. For instance, notices will say 25% off, or a free cup of coffee, or a voucher worth twenty euro with every two items sold, or whatever it is on the day, or for a particular period of time.

Sales are all about communicating with people, providing value for money and benefits to the user, and the platforms from which products or services are promoted. Where people buy, and what people buy is influenced by factors such as familiarity, trust, recommendations, price, personal needs, preferences, spending priorities and economic factors. Recommendations have entered a new phase through online communication tools which facilitate social media such as blogging and twittering, and websites dedicated to feedback on particular areas, for example, hotel stays and new products. One of the factors contributing to the success of social media is that it facilitates communities of people to present and exchange views and experiences. It empowers people with a voice and a speed of communication which, in turn, has the potential to influence others. Social media and social networking have become part of the communications landscape for individuals, business and organizations.

Section 2

Marketing

Introduction

There is no point in starting a business if you keep it a secret! Firstly, you have to decide who your targeted customers are. Once you know that, they would be captured in your marketing campaign through you targeting the appropriate market segment. The characteristics, values, and habits of your customer type are jointly referred to as your customer profile information.

A market segment represents those buyers in the market place who will respond to your product in a similar way, because it will meet their needs - be that a basic need and/or one of appreciation of the benefit and value of your product or service in their lives. This market information and your own resources (financial, time, personnel, product, etc) will guide you as to how best to communicate information to your potential and/or current customers, which will form the basis of your marketing plan. You also need to be clear about the message you want to communicate to your target customers, in other words, what your business is offering them, and the benefits. You will need a marketing plan, no matter what business or level of resources you possess.

The complexity of marketing

Marketing is a complex communication operation that takes clearly defined messages to targeted customers who reside in targeted market places. These can be local, national, international or global, or a combination of some or all of these. Marketing communicates the message that you wish to deliver, for example - that you have a product or service available to benefit the recipient and/or their extended circle. It also communicates the visual - what the product/ service looks or feels like, and portrays the social innuendo through brand and price association as well as the benefits of its use. It also - directly or indirectly - communicates a positive image about the company. In addition, the style of the marketing tools used represent part of this often subliminal message.

Online marketing

The internet, particularly email, has become a cost-effective marketing medium. Email messages have also the facility to send links to websites, and to carry attachments such as large documents, photographs, and video foot- age. However, the data protection laws give the receiver the right to opt out of receiving further emails from you/your business. To become more aware of online user rights in Ireland, perhaps visit the Irish Data Protection website[1].

Really Simple Syndication feeds (RSS) and Widgets are relatively new devel- opments. RSS are feeds of data which are activated by an embedded widget located, normally, either online or on your computer desktop. This combined system allows single or multiple streams of information, such as blogs, adver- tising, news or other information, to be downloaded. It means that you can arrange to have convenient access to your favourite sites or information of particular interest. The widget is an embedded code that operates like a web- site within a website. Widgets can be tracked by the sender, so if you forward a widget to your online community (social networking), then an opportunity to make money presents itself when someone buys a product as a result. In these instances, you could receive a referral fee. So these tools have come to be included in marketing strategies.

Online marketing has become a key way of promoting your business brand, products, and services. The three main online marketing strategies include:-

---

1   http://www.dataprotection.ie/docs/Home/4.htm

   i.   Search engine marketing (SEM[1])
   ii. Search engine optimization (SEO)
   iii. Google AdWords

i.   Search engine marketing (SEM) forms part of the dynamics of internet marketing. It endeavours to increase the presence of the site (be it a website or a networking site link) in search engine result pages through the use of such tools as Search Engine Optimization (SEO), paid placement, contextual advertising and paid inclusion.

ii. Search engine optimization (SEO) is regarded as an organic facility, ie no advertising cost. It is a process of achieving a high listing of the site/ networking link as a result of searches via the internet. It is a process of analysing the site, its users and competitors and building key terms into the site design which will naturally result in it being listed on particular search paths.

iii. Google Adwords[2] is a form of advertising service offered by Google. An advert, commonly referred to as a sponsored link, is produced, and located on the side of the main screen page. This is a very low cost and effective form of advertising, as you only pay when a customer clicks on your link (advert). The advert is activated when associated words are entered into the Google search engine.

Online media and communication tools

Developments in online capabilities have changed the sales marketing dynamic to the extent that the receiver of the information (the consumer/potential consumer in particular) now has a voice to respond, and has the power to influence a wide community. However, some standard marketing concepts, such as segmentation, are still as relevant as ever and have even become integrated into some new online media such as blogging.

For instance, when you register online as a blogger, you are advised to narrow your area of interest to achieve greater impact. This compares to direct marketing, where the audience is identified and becomes a particular targeted segment within the market place. Segmentation means that marketing spend

---

1   http://en.wikipedia.org/wiki/Search_engine_marketing
2   www.Google.ie/AdWords

results in a high positive response rate, and the brand is not damaged by being relegated to the status of 'spam' by the uninterested.

For many people, blogging began as a hobby or fun thing to do. Now, many bloggers have progressed into the mainstream media arena and are formally consulted by other media or businesses for their views, due to their influence within their respective online communities. A forum is similar to a blog but operates within a more select (by choice) community. Software that facilitates internet users to create their own blog sites is also available free online to download.

Social media, as an online communication medium, has proliferated to older age groups due to its influence across a multitude of sectors within society. Always pushing out the boundaries, and creating excitement for current and potential users, social media cannot be ignored. It facilitates the sharing of information, views, comments, experiences, photographs, music and video. Relevant examples of social media are: Facebook.com, Twitter.com, Flickr.com, foursquare.com, muzu.tv.com, YouTube.com, Last.fm.com and LinkedIn.com. Social forums include Boards.ie

YouTube is a video-sharing website; Facebook offers both personal and business pages to host details and email exchange; Last.fm is a network for music fans; and LinkedIn was setup for professionals to interact with each other.

For any business, social media networks can provide valuable feedback on what is being said about their business, their market place, about people's needs and views in general. They can also be consulted for feedback. Twitter, for example, can be used by businesses as a source of consumer information, customer service, and/or part of a brand management strategy. While it is frowned upon to openly promote your product or service online on twitter in a brash fashion, you can use it to respond to any comments made about your business or brand.

Social networking offers opportunities for people and businesses to enter into conversations and build communities. Consumer Protection, through Unfair Trading Regulations 2008, made it illegal for anyone to pose as a consumer in order to benefit their trade, business, craft or profession. This new legislation brought greater transparency and trust to social networking.

One hears much of the concept of the power of the crowd. This explains the reality that potential buyers and users of services often go online to pose a question or look for reports on people's previous experiences before they make a decision to commit to any purchase. Many review-focused websites offer a grading system where the person can score their experience – be it with a brand of shampoo, a mortgage provider, or a hotel stay. People often visit forums, such as Boards.ie, to seek advice. For example: How do I go about exporting to China? The online community empowers the consumer with a voice, the power to respond, and has become an influencing power within the market place, government, social and other organizations as well as people's homes. It has grown to become a global village of easy conversations.

The multi-user email pooling system, better known as twitter, can be helpful and swift in warning against scams in the market place, which includes online. You can also do an internet search using a search engine such as Google.com on a person or business. To search for scams, simply input the word 'scams' or 'recent scams' and view the listing results that the search produces. In general, be careful and realise that you represent yourself and/ or your organization when you participate in the social networks (in fact any communication), so be aware of your own brand image and be aware that trust is something that you generate by your actions and words.

The use of the internet's range of facilities, for personal or business benefit, are as wide and limited as a user's understanding and strategic mindset. Thinking outside the box and keeping yourself up to date with what is happening will broaden your perspective. Relevant newspaper supplements and magazines, on areas such as business, banking and financial markets, marketing, technology, science and legal issues, will help you to keep your finger on the pulse of economic activity and spot potential development for your business. Most publications have an online presence and publish articles online. Being aware of public, political and industry opinions is important, and even more so if you are a global business and/or wish to develop in that direction.

Market segmentation

As a business start-up, you will probably focus on a particular market segment, in other words, a particular customer type. This is the most effective strategy, as it is more likely to deliver a speedier return on investment, i.e. sales (turnover), and thus income, as a result of your niche marketing campaign. Market segmentation is the division of the potential consumer sales into different categories according to certain criteria. Essentially they can be defined under three descriptive categories, as follows:-

i. Demographic
ii. Geographic
iii. Behavioural

i.   Demographic: describes the profile of the customers, for example, age, sex, income, occupation, education, events celebrated and attended, race and ethnic origin.

ii.   Geographic: describes customers in terms of where they are located.

iii. Behavioural: describes how people behave with regard to the purchase and use of a given category of goods and services.

In today's world of global media, product and service innovations and the high consumer need for constant change and excitement, any insightful and innovative market segmentation can bring speedy success to marketing campaigns. A business can identify a common set of factors that create and bond a group, and differentiates them from others. The business can then specify the criteria which identifies that segment. This segment is quantified, i.e. the volume of sales and growth potential in that market segment can be estimated. Planning how you are going to inform that group/people about your product or service is one part of a marketing strategy.

It is through market research that organizations find potential customer types.

Market research

There are market research companies which perform this function, however, as a start-up, you may wish to do your own research. So it is up to you to research how best you approach this, and/or you could always talk to colleagues, students of marketing, or post a question in the online Boards.ie forum.
There are two basic types of market research:-

i. Primary
ii. Secondary

i.   **Primary research**: is where you initiate and implement research specifically for your own business. Perhaps the cheapest for a start-up would be to devise a Questionnaire and distribute it by email, hand or post. However, you would need to initially invite participation.

ii   **Secondary research:** is the collection of information from sources such as articles, books, case studies on other similar businesses and internet searches.

The Questionaire presents a wonderful opportunity to promote you and/or your business to potential customers and receive feedback. If using hardcopies of the Questionnaire, then you must ensure that they have a self-addressed envelope (with stamp). Perhaps, include a business card with the Questionnaire.

The Questionnaire must be carefully planned. Questions should reflect all key aspects of your business. Examples could be: the mode of delivery service, payment details, the product or service itself, and the client's preferences in using a product/service such as you are offering.Other questions could be: if privacy is important, personal attention, if price matters, how your product or service would rate relative to other similar services, what key factors would retain their custom, and by what means could they be targeted in an advertising/marketing campaign. You should list choices, for example, internet, mobile phone, television, local or national radio, flyer, local newspaper, national newspaper, magazines, or outdoor advertising such as bus, bus stop or bill boards. It is up to you the entrepreneur to consider how best you can target your potential and current customers. However, there are occasions when the customer profile may end up being different to what you had planned, so be flexible and keep an open mind while making your footprints along your chosen path/s.

As your customer base grows, you may operate a loyalty card or club card system. If so, the information taken from application forms is among the sources of consumer data that helps businesses to get to know the type of consumer using their services and/or shopping with them. This is a relatively inexpensive means of market research. However, to encourage customers to complete the forms, an incentive is normally offered, such as discounts, vouchers or entry into a prize-draw.

The fundamental principles of marketing

The 4 Ps are the keystone-pillars around which the principles of traditional marketing revolve:-

i.   Product
ii. Price
iii. Place
iv. Promotion

i.   Product
Your product and/or service must be defined clearly. You need to consider criteria such as whether the quality, design and price of your product/service reflect your target customers and your position in the market place. Customer needs and customer lifestyle are two key factors when assessing the market potential for your product/service. So it is important to be able to define your product or service and any other value added benefit that you provide. If you have competitors in the market place, then analyse, on an ongoing basis, how you can gain advantages over them through offering added benefits and value. This is known as gaining competitive advantage.

ii. Price
You need to be aware of the prices of similar competitor products/services in your market place, the availability of substitutes for your product/service, and the differential value (comparative advantage) provided by your product or service relative to those of your competitors. Also, you have to consider your own costs of production, for example, your buying power from wholesalers, your costs of distribution, costs of providing an after-sale service, your target sales volume, profit margin, and costs of marketing and sales promotion to maintain and increase sales. These are some of the key factors that you will consider when you are setting your price.

Also, the price will affect your brand image, and the higher it is, the more exclusive it becomes as fewer people can afford it. So your target customer (market segment) and the profile of your product/service (brand image) will greatly influence your pricing strategy. As a start-up, and/or when you are developing a new line of business, there can be an element of luck in the timing of your market entry. Having a flexible approach will allow you to review and adjust your pricing and business strategy, as you continue to make your footprints along your path.

Pricing is a challenging and vitally important part of any business success strategy. However, changes in the economic situation of customers due to, for example, an economic downturn or upturn, can have a direct impact upon the consumption of goods and services. Consumers become more or less discerning with regards to how they spend their money in response to changes in economic conditions. So, in either downturns or up-turns, companies need to consider revising aspects of their business operation. This can open doors to creating value-added benefits to their products/services such as competitions, discount or other promotional opportunities, or produce opportunities for new product lines and/or new services.

iii. Place

Planning your distribution well can strongly influence your market share. So, some questions you need to consider are: where will your product/service be available, where will the channels of distribution be located, will you have a website providing information, and what is your opportunity for online sales. If you intend to use a warehouse, which stock-management system will you use and how will you operate it. If you are offering a luxury product/service, you need to be located or available in locations that reflect the image of your product and brand, and also reflect the type of locations frequented by your typical customer. Being innovative will allow you to review what is available and consider other ways of making your product/service available for sale.

iv. Promotion

Promotion is all about communicating a positive message to your targeted customer. It can be done by using tools such as advertising, sales promotion, personal selling and publicity. Sales promotion tends to be a short-term effort to increase sales. It is also used to inform and entice people to test new-to-the-market products and/or services. Personal selling is best used when working with a small niche market, as it allows for discussion, clarification and feedback on what is being offered, and on customer needs and benefits. The advertising of promotions can be scaled up to mass media, such as national television, radio or press; or local, such as newspapers, newsletters or radio, and, in some areas, a cable television service. The platforms for promotion purposes have broadened due to new facilities available online as well as on the mobile phone. Email, and email with video, and website attachments, YouTube, website advertising, social networking, e-newsletters, widgets and Apps are among the new promotion platforms available.

Branding

Branding is a big issue in product and service development and positioning in the market place. A brand presents an exclusive recognition factor. It differentiates a business offering from competitors. If managed successfully, it can create long-term value, maintain and grow sales, and people/businesses will wish to be associated with it. A brand can be any combination of name, symbol or design, and can also be legally protected under intellectual property rights legislation. (For more detail, see legal and business, Part 7). A brand helps build loyalty and repeat purchases, and adds value to both business and product lines. Well known Irish brands include: Dunnes Stores, Kerrygold, Dairygold, Lily O'Briens, Waterford Glass, Flahavan's Progress Oatlets, Odlums, Barry's Tea, Insomnia, Smithwicks, Aer Lingus, Ryan Air, and Aer Arann.

However, brands must be managed and updated, because trends in the market change and customers today need regular change and excitement. Marketing is a key tool in the establishment, promotion and maintenance of brand value. A successful brand means that you can extend the brand to other products/services. You will have to do less marketing to lure new customers, as the recognition of the brand by customers, and its reputation, helps to establish trust and confidence in the new launch. A successful brand receives respect from all associated with the business, such as suppliers, wholesalers, retailers, distributors, customers, marketing agencies, the media, etc.

As a start-up or young business, the design of your business card, stationary, email, and the style of advertising communication, even how you present yourself to your customer, are all part of the image of your business and together they contribute to brand creation. A successful brand may also play a part, long-term, in facilitating the franchising of your business, should you decide to go down that route.

What markets should you target?

The four basic markets that a company may consider are:-

    i.   Niche
   ii.   Mass market
  iii.   Global
  iv.   Growth market

The entrepreneur must also consider what the market will want in three to five years time. Factors to consider include changes in customer needs or trends, new competitors into the market place, political, economic or technological changes. It is not an easy task but to stay in business it is necessary to be forward looking, flexible, and to keep your destination in mind. One helpful indicator is to observe the trends happening in your sector in other countries as it can inspire you but can also pre-empt what could happen in your own market place.

i.   Niche markets

It is more common for small businesses to target more narrow market areas. This strategy avoids being in direct competition with mass market-driven competitors, who have greater resources available to them. These include the factors of production, distribution, marketing, customer service etc., and for these reasons, normally, small start-up businesses tend to focus on niche areas not mass markets.

Targeting specific market segments is the most economical and successful marketing path for a young business to follow. You may decide to target a sector at a local level, national, and/or international level. Make sure that you can meet the demand if the reaction to your marketing campaign is positive. Accumulating a back-log of orders is bad for business. Being unable to meet the demand for your product/service without long delays, will lessen your opportunity for repeat business, create a bad reputation for your business and could result in cancelled orders. You would need to have a system set up to cope with high volume orders, should that happen, or decide to grow your sales and business slowly and steadily.

Every entrepreneur will find their own path and must use their own instincts, and not allow either ego or pride become confused with instinct. Innovative footprints will be made by some entrepreneurs. Others will follow more traditional marketing strategies and standard segmentation/s. New products and services should create new markets. Every new market entry offers potential for creating new market segmentations. One way to find a new market is to look for disruption in the current market place, and look for changes or needs in all areas, such as business, education, consumer, social and public services. Then look at your skills, and what you can make happen. Then let your eye and heart for entrepreneurship take hold.

ii.   Mass markets

The two basic types are either with or without market segmentation. The segmentation method is where you create a different product for different market segments, and produce a separate marketing campaign for each market segment. In this process, every segment is targeted, but it is time consuming, labour intensive, and very expensive. The mass market approach without market segmentation is where you generate one product or service and one marketing campaign and direct it to everyone. However, it is generally perceived that the mass market approach combined with market segmentation is the more effective, but does demand a much bigger investment on all levels.

iii. Global markets

If you wish to mass market internationally then carefully consider the pitfalls. In particular, study your financial resources, as taking on too many countries too quickly without sufficient resources, may cause your downfall. Do not forget that there are differences in countries across many areas, which include different cultures and attitudes, different legislation, taxation, trade arrangements, technical standards, and even different perceptions of successful advertising standards. These differences can cause a mass marketing strategy to fail.

You may need a different marketing campaign for some countries, to provide for differences in time, language, technical standards, and other cultural and business differences. So you can see the importance of carrying out research in new markets, particularly if there are already no competitors providing similar services or products. Be aware that a competitor may enter your new-found market. Intellectual Property Rights can protect you from having parts or all elements of your product or service reproduced for commercial purposes by other parties.

iv. Growth markets

A business that wishes to produce high volume sales and grow their market share quickly, will adopt this business model if at all possible. This type of strategy appeals to strong niche market products or services which are derived by serious research and development, and marketing capabilities, and tend to result in economic indicators showing sustainable sales and growth.

A lot of the dot.com businesses adopted this approach. Also, if you are interested in attracting a business angel or business investor, then this is the best possible plan to take, as investors tend to look for a 30% to 60% return on investment over a relatively short period of time, such as three to five years, and growth markets tend to provide relatively quick and high returns.

Competitive advantage

As you enter a new market with your product or service, it is imperative to your survival that you have some competitive advantage over other competitors in the market place. Price alone is not enough to sustain your place in the market, as so often the larger business operators will lower their prices or offer promotional deals to push you out of the market simply by luring your customers away. The bigger company will be able to sustain a loss on particular product lines for a period of time. In contrast, a small company will quickly run out of cash and will not be able to afford to run at a loss for any extended period of time. So you need to focus on offering some value other than price to your target customers.

Why use a marketing agency?

If you do not have marketing experience, and/or do not feel confident about managing the marketing of your own business, then you should consider using the services of a professional marketing agency. Selecting a suitable one for your business is important. It would be time well spent to set up a provisional appointment with a number of marketing agencies who have experience of dealing with clients involved in your industry/sector. In your communication to them (phone, email or letter) advise them that you require a provisional consultation prior to giving them your business. This initial meeting is to ensure that you feel comfortable with the agency's people and believe that they understand your business, your marketing needs, and will work within your marketing budget.

Marketing agencies may have their own areas of expertise, so you have to do your research to find the one that best fits your business and personality needs. Marketing agencies will have a wide range of experience, gained from working with other companies, to bring to your business. They will know the different customer profiles and how best to reach them. They will present to you their best suggestions on the most suitable brand and image for your business. They will possess the tools and know-how to achieve this for you. They will want you to succeed, as then you will continue to do business with them, and your success as a client will impact upon their profile as a successful marketing agency.

The benefits of marketing

Social networking, as a marketing facility, is low cost, particularly if you do it yourself. The other option is to engage an online marketing specialist agency or person. Social networking may not capture your target customers. Sometimes a mix of media tools make for the best marketing strategy as, it communicates your message to the range of consumer types. As a start-up, it is not always possible to have total knowledge of the customers groups which may be interested in what your business is offering. So allowing for additional take-up and increasing awareness outside of your target group makes sense. Word of mouth is also a strong communication tool, and should not be over-looked. There are many times when marketing will seem like an invisible investment, as it does not create a product or service.

In summary, marketing performs a wide range of functions, including the following:-
- informing people of the benefits and value of the product/service
- creating an image of the user of the product/service
- endorsing the brand and promoting the image of the business
- empowering the customer to make their own value judgements on the product/service
- increasing the recognition value (be it online or in stores) resulting in deliberate and impulse buys
- informing potential distributors and agents of your product/service
- increasing the trust factor in the product/service
- creating a need in the potential customer to try the product/service

Section 3

Public Relations (PR)

Introduction

Often, people confuse marketing with public relations (PR). They are as different as a Doctor of Psychology (Psychologist) is different to a Medical Doctor (General Practitioner). Marketing promotes and manages the communication of information on products and services, with a view to increasing sales, and creating and maintaining a brand presence in the market place. Public relations is about a company involving itself in campaigns and activities which directly and/or indirectly create and maintain goodwill and understanding with their clients, customers, potential customers and, in general, with members of the public, government bodies and other organizations.

However, those involved in PR should communicate with the people involved in the marketing side to ensure continuity, and vice versa. For example, the same branding and image of the company should be used in both the PR and the marketing campaigns. Branding and image and the core message are among the areas where PR and marketing must overlap to ensure continuity of the company's core message. A core message might be, a luxury branded service provider, a cheap and cheerful store, or a 24-hour efficient international service. Also, it is necessary to ensure that the colours representing the company's branding are used in all the communications, promotion and display material associated with all events and activities across the company.

PR agencies promote and manage information messages for a wide range of clients. These include businesses, voluntary organizations, government offices, individuals, the media, and sometime can include competitors, with a view to creating and maintaining a positive image. PR aims to ensure a positive uptake on information in the public sphere in general. Some PR agencies specialise in an area such as event management, promotions, sponsorship, financial/corporate affairs, and international services. Others offer a wide range of expertise, and most will help you to prepare a strategy in the event of different eventualities such as damage limitation in a time of crisis, which for a business can impact negatively upon reputation, sales, business value, and staff morale. For a public company, negative publicity normally decreases share value. In general, journalists are supposed to write and report articles with relative objectivity. On the other hand, PR professionals write the press releases and present the news story with a damage limitation bias for the people or business they are representing. Press releases are released to the media for reporting upon or not, as the case may be. They tend to be sent by email or fax, as post is relatively slow by comparison.

Online PR is a growing practice. There is an increased awareness among industry sectors, of the power of social networking. With more start-ups emerging, and the relative low cost of online circulation, there is no doubt that online PR will continue to reach out to, and be engaged by, an increasing number of businesses into the future.

The power of public relations

As a start-up or developing business, effective use of PR and being aware of its power takes time, thought, and practice. Possessing some expertise and PR skills will help the entrepreneur to handle most situations to the best advantage of the business. Effective PR is about building relationships around trust. It is about profile building for the long-term.

Some tips for entrepreneurs in particular would be to become involved in your local community, let people know what you are doing. If you are a good speaker and have enthusiasm for a particular area then get yourself onto local radio, in local newspapers, or get letters published in national newspapers. There are opportunities for you to promote yourself as the entrepreneur, and, as respect for you grows, it may generate business leads. You are the most informed judge of what is best for your business and your target customers. Always retain self-respect if you wish to be taken seriously as a business person, and to be trusted and respected. Building the business profile is not just about the product and service, but about how business is transacted with all who engage with it, from staff and new recruits, to contractors, suppliers, manufacturers, agents, distributors, customers, and the local community in which the business operates. PR is about establishing and maintaining successful relationships. Social networking is also a useful tool for keeping your presence alive in the minds of communities, and for keeping a finger on the pulse of conversations and consumer trends that reflect and represent your market segment. Many businesses now have a presence on Facebook, but take a visit before you sign up. If you join, and later decide to withdraw from the system, your files will be stored and may remain the property of Facebook. Always remember that everything you say can be taken to reflect you, the person, and you, the entrepreneur, and may impact upon whether people will do business with you in the short and/or long-term.

How to manage in a crisis

A crisis management PR plan is normally prepared as a precautionary measure. It means that you, along with your key management and staff, have a procedure in place should a crisis situation happen involving your business. Appointing a spokesperson (yourself or another) helps to avoid inappropriate and/or conflicting information being reported to the media and other bodies. The appointed spokesperson must undergo some induction as to the procedures to follow, and be given a list of appropriate contact numbers. In fact, all staff should have the contact number for the spokesperson. The spokesperson should have the expertise to limit the damage as far as possible. Often, a crisis situation can be turned around to demonstrate the ethics or stamina of the business or the owner/s. For example, it could show that customer care is the company's number one priority, or that the wellbeing of staff is paramount to the company's success. Alternatively, the company's actions, for example, a product withdrawal due to a reported defect, can reflect the company policy of achieving standards of excellence in their product/service.

A SWOT analysis

A PR plan is a fundamental part of any campaign undertaken by a PR professional. This can only be done with the full assistance of the main business driver, which, in this case, is the business entrepreneur, you! The research, vision and time put into the development of this plan will help to prioritise whatever action needs to be taken to set and achieve goals. The PR plan is commonly referred to as the SWOT analysis. It examines the business and market place under these headings: strengths (S), weaknesses (W), opportunities (O), and threats (T). The result guides the PR Plan. It will result in a suitable campaign being planned which sets out to achieve the aims of the business.

Sponsorship

Sponsorship provides a financing opportunity for many events and activities. You can be a sponsor or engage a sponsor.

You can find a sponsor and engage them to fund some event or activity, which you either cannot afford to do yourself or choose not to fund from your limited resources. Sponsorship can create opportunities to work with other people/businesses, and it can hold the potential to open up new opportunities. Sometimes having a well established name as your sponsor adds credibility and trust to the activity. The sponsor is normally an outside organization, business or individual that takes full or part responsibility for the settlement of the costs involved with an event, activity or undertaking. In return the sponsor often has their name, brand, product or service associated with the event, activity or undertaking, by means of having it incorporated into the title. As part of the sponsorship deal, it can be agreed that the sponsor also has an opportunity to show or print information about its products or services, and promote that directly or indirectly to the targeted and/or attending public. Every sponsorship deal is individually negotiated. So, just because you secure a sponsor, do not be so grateful that you allow them to take over your show! The sponsor can be given options depending upon how much he decides to invest in the sponsorship deal. Always have your options worked out in advance of approaching a sponsor. Know the benefits that you are selling in return for sponsorship, and negotiate with the potential sponsor. Do not decide to think on your feet as you may end up giving away more benefit than you get for your sponsorship deal.

Companies sponsor events of all sorts, from trade shows and art exhibitions to sporting events and sports teams and/or their sports wear. They also sponsor broadcast programmes, publication costs, as well as community, business and education initiatives. Sponsorship opportunities are as limited as your imagination. The benefit to the business, organization or person offering the sponsorship is, most often, to be publicly associated with the event or activity. It heightens the business or organization's profile, gains customer loyalty, and establishes and maintains good relationships with all stakeholders and the community in which they are located. Sponsorship of radio or television programmes requires substantial investment. They are expensive media in which to advertise, but the return on your investment i.e. exposure to a high volume of listeners/viewers, can be rewarding. In most cases, deals are negotiated. In the broadcast world, a full programme sponsor is allocated advertising time, or stings which play into and out of the programme during the breaks. They may have their brand mentioned during the programme, and the sponsor is mentioned in publicity material associated with the programme. Sponsorship opportunities can provide innovative opportunities for businesses to gain publicity.

As a start-up, it is likely that instead of giving money to sponsor any event or activity, you would offer your skills, time, or some other facility in order to assist.

Be innovative

One should always think three to five years ahead in order to maintain an advantage over the competition. This can be achieved by focusing on new ways of doing things in order to reduce costs, or develop new products or services to satisfy future consumer needs. However, as an entrepreneur, if you are working alone, it is challenging enough to focus on the present and the multi-dimensions involved in business and still possess the mental capacity and energy to think about future developments.

Time management is key. Realise that you cannot expect to do all things in any one day or week. If you try to do everything at once, then you will most likely fail, so schedule your things to do in a realistic time frame. Have a schedule that allows you a day or two off, now and again, to chill out. It is also important to attend conferences or trade shows related to your industry, to broaden your perspective. These visits will be part of the process of keeping you informed and in touch with others within, and associated with your area of business. It will help to keep you up to date with developments in technology, which could impact upon business operations for you and/or your competitors.

In addition, subscribing to journals or newsletters (hardcopy or online) will also help to keep you informed of developments and new thinking. Staying in business is all about people and keeping in touch, and, of course, cash flow management! Every time you go out you should have a business card in your pocket. Every time you send an email, your company details and a short mission statement should be tagged onto your email. It is all part of the marketing and PR processes which never sleep!

Use your individuality to make a difference in how you operate and grow your business!

Bibi's choice

A selection of business terms explained

Differentiation: the qualities that present differences between similar products or services.

Competitive Advantage: The qualities that make your product or service stand out ahead of your competitors' products or services.

Substitute Product: A similar product that could be purchased as an alternative to the one currently being sold.

Telephone Marketing: Using the telephone to contact current and potential customers to inform them of your products/services with a view to inducing sales.

E-marketing: Using the internet services to contact current and potential customers. Companies often put their website address on their literature and packaging. It encourages people to visit and find information on current and new product ranges, and on the business itself. Emails are often sent with company messages and company contacts listed. Also, if you have a website for your business, (which is highly recommended) then there is the opportunity to get a listing on google.com. It is possible to ensure that your company is listed in the first few pages when someone enters any of the key words linked to your website into the search engine. However, while Google offers this service, there is a charge for it.

Viral Web Marketing: This is any marketing initiative (formal or informal) that encourages website users to forward the electronic message (email, content, or website link) to a number of other people, thus expanding the number of people viewing the message. Social networking, and the use of Really Simple Syndication (RSS) feeds and Widgets, has also expanded this dynamic platform.

Direct Marketing: Directly contacting the customer with the aim of building a relationship and securing sales. Some examples are: email; e-newsletter; the direct distribution of flyers, leaflets, brochures; and telephone cold calling to customers. RSS and Widgets are now part of the direct marketing strategy, as are Apps for mobile phones (iphones).

Social Bookmarking: this is an online social networking tool that allows the user to share links to content on web pages.

Speaking from experience

Entrepreneur: Denis O'Brien

The key to opportunity is to have an open mind - successful entrepreneurs will focus on every last detail. They will do everything to minimize the risks and maximize the potential.

Research is vital - of the product, the markets, the costs, the competition. Self-belief is very important together with identifying the right team. Pursuing a business opportunity can be a lonely route...putting all your energy, effort and money on the line. But there are successful entrepreneurs who will help and give advice and it is important to keep well away from people who are constantly negative. Optimists are the best at seeing opportunities.

Over time the employment of 2 or 3 people can expand into 10 and then 100 employees ....that is how businesses succeed and grow.

Your courage, vision, determination and persistence are the traits which will carry you on your journey.

Denis O'Brien, Digicel Group/Communicorp Group Ltd

PART 7

LEGAL AND BUSINESS

- Introduction

Section 1
- Business formation options

Section 2
- Is the franchise business model for you?

Section 3
- Intellectual property rights

Section 4
- How to register as self-employed

Section 5
- The employment of staff and contract workers

Section 6
- Why take out professional indemnity insurance

.egal and Business

ntroduction

When setting up a business, there are a number of areas that need to be considered, researched, and legally put in place by you. You will require the services of a solicitor, in some cases. These form part of the early business planning and formation. It is an exciting period for any entrepreneur. It is a time when decisions have to be made and, in some instances, contracts have to be signed which are legally binding. It is good practice to organize an opt-out clause where it is at all possible, even if you think you will never need to use it. Legal requirements vary from country to country, within and outside of the European Union, and are also dependent upon your business type and the description of your products or services.

If you are trading in Ireland, the law requires you to register a business name. Every trading company must register and file tax returns to the Government's Revenue Department, at the end of the financial year, even if you are exempt or have a zero sum tax liability. If you plan on operating a business from your home, you would need to read your property contract and/or discretely contact the relevant local authority to discover if you are limited in the type of business, if any, that you can operate from your home. Residential (zoning) requirements may exist that limit or control the use of residential property for business operations. If you are seeking a particular license to operate a certain type of business, a safety inspection may be required as part of the application process.

In relation to insurance, you should consider third party fire and theft, and maybe third party liability. This guards you against possible personal financial loss and/or the depletion of the funds within your company/business, should a client or supplier happen to become injured while on your property and make a claim against you for injury. Also, if you engage staff, ensure they are also covered against injury in the performance of their duties both on and off your property. Every employer has a duty of care to their workers, so it is required that you give them instructions on health and safety matters in relation to your business. (For more on insurance, see Part 5)

Health and safety regulations may also impact upon your business. Some products and services such as alcohol, pharmaceuticals, and ammunitions, operate under heavy government, European Union and other international regulations.

You should research well the limits that exist on your chosen business product or service, starting with the country in which your business will operate. Also, there may be legal requirements for the countries with which you wish to deal. Researching information can be slow, but if you do it right the first time, and keep informed of changes in legislation which directly affect your business and your business operations, then you will have little to worry about, so long as you comply with the rules and regulations and file your tax returns on time! Due to internet services such as search engines, websites, email, networking sites and forums, there are many sources of information for the emerging entrepreneur.

Section 1

Business formation options

When you are starting a business, you need to consider how you will structure it. The sole trader and company are the two most popular options. This will be dictated by factors such as: the control you wish to have over your business, the type of business, the liability protection that you require, the number of people involved, and the future expansion possibilities that you envisage. If you intend doing business exclusively online, then unless you are a .com, you only need to register a business name. If the business grows and you wish to take on a partner and/or investors, then you may need to consider a legal entity and/or involve detailed contracts in order to adequately document and protect all involved in the business.

Below is a list of the business structures and not-for-profit options. From these, you need to consider which is best for you. The next step is completing and signing the formal documentation, which legally sets up your business formation (or your not-for-profit organization). When this is signed by the solicitor and the parties involved in the business, it must be lodged with the appropriate government body. The main business structure options are:-

   i.   Sole Trader
   ii.   Partnership
  iii.   Private Limited Company (Ltd)
  iv.   Public Limited Company (Plc)
   v.   Cooperative
  vi.   Charity

i.   Sole trader

This involves just one person: the owner. It is the simplest form of business structure. A sole trader is not legally protected, as the owner can lose whatever has been invested into the business, and can be held personally liable for any debts incurred by it. Nevertheless, because of the simplicity of its structure, it is a popular choice of business structure for small start-up entrepreneurs. As sole trader business ownerships tend to be small, the liability concerns are immediately greatly diminished, particularly in comparison to large companies who deal in transactions worth millions. The sole trader must register a business name. The sole trader should buy public liability insurance to protect against a claim should anyone have an accident or become injured on the premises. Working from home has less risk, but if suppliers visit or you yourself wish to be insured against injury, then it is worth investigating the insurance options and costs.
(For more on insurance, see Part 5).

ii.   Partnership

This is a legal bond where a number of persons numbering, normally, between 2 and 20 (this number can be exceeded for professionals), come together to carry on a business with the common aim of making a profit. It is a common form of business formation for professionals such as solicitors, doctors, veterinary practitioners, accountants, and computer professionals.

iii.   Limited company

The private limited company is a common business structure, where the business has a separate legal identity from its owners/shareholders. However, company law is not universal. You will need to check out the legal requirements in the country in which your business is registered and where your business is located. A private company is any company not defined as a public company.

iv.   Public company

A public company can have their shares listed on the stock exchange and must comply with regulations. This business structure requires that business and monetary regulations are met, before being considered for a listing on any stock exchange. Public companies normally release shares as a call for capital investment (a money injection) in return for a share in the ownership of the business (equity). This is not an option for consideration for small or start-up businesses, but is included here for your information.

v.   Cooperative

A cooperative is a voluntary group of like-minded people who have decided to collectively undertake tasks for themselves. It is a jointly owned and democratically run organization. There are many different types of cooperatives, and these vary with regards to their legal requirements from country to country. There is no one legal requirement for a cooperative internationally. Factors which strongly influence the legal formation include: the legal requirements of the country in which it will be based, the type of business, and the number of people involved. In Ireland, there are different types of cooperatives, but to date, they have been focused around agriculture and finance. In other countries cooperatives have been formally set up to fill gaps within the community in the areas of education, childcare, housing, and environmental protection.

Comment: perhaps this will become more prevalent in Ireland and worldwide over the coming years, as the weakness of capitalism, which contributed to the recession of 2008, has caused a search for a more sustainable way of working.

vi.   Charity

If running a business is not for you, but you wish to be involved with similar dynamics, then you might consider setting up a charity or voluntary group. However, every voluntary body needs to have a structure in order to operate in an organized and efficient manner. The scope, goals and activities, and long-term plans of the group will dictate how it should best be organized. Every voluntary organization needs to be creative in how it goes about its activities. For example, running a charity includes planning, operations management, public relations, marketing, communication, accounting, technology management, and the required legal framework has to be set up and managed.

There are often strict requirements for the setting up of a charity which differ from state to state/country to country. For instance, in Ireland, the Government's Revenue Office is responsible for granting voluntary organisations a charity status, and allocates successful applicants a particular CHY number. This registration number is officially recognised and bestows a charity status upon the organisation. This, in turn, exempts the organization from various taxes, such as DIRT and income tax. In addition, if it operates as a corporate identity (company legal structure), the charity is also excluded from paying corporation tax. This charity (CHY) number must be quoted on all stationary and correspondence. This is the only official register of charities in Ireland, unlike the UK, which has a charity commission for England and Wales that sets down clear criteria for the operation and management of a charity, including annual returns, accounts, details of trustees, and annual updates.

ection 2

s the franchise business model for you?

A franchise can be a perfect way for an entrepreneur to launch in the market place with an already established and recognized business identity. This business format is where an already established and successful trading company creates a facility where another person can buy in to repeat the same business format, using the same operating systems and branding. The originator of the business (franchisor) receives a normally substantial start-up payment and a percentage of the profit for the duration of the lease of the franchise. The franchisor is the person who develops the franchise business format. The franchisee is the person who takes on the obligation to run a repeat of the business format, as specified by the franchisor.

A franchise can be anything from a dry cleaning business or grocery store, to a printing shop, coffee house or art gallery. It can be any business at all that has proven itself over a period of years to be profitable. It can be either service or product driven, or both. Not any business can become a franchise operator. A business should have proven itself to be a trading success over a number of years before it considers establishing a franchise for lease. However, remember that just because a business is successful in one country or state or area, it does not mean that it will be successful in another area. Different countries will vary on regulations for both home franchise and those for export. O'Brien's Sandwich Bars, SuperValu, Centra, SPAR, Londis, Maxol (Mace), are examples of well known Irish franchises, some of which have franchisees outside of Ireland.

There is always an element of risk when you take on a franchise. However, the tendency is that if the business represents a recognised brand with a high success rate in other areas, and if the standard of living is similar in the planned new area, then the likelihood of success is high. There are no guarantees, and the outlay for a franchise is relatively high, so do your research if you decide to go down that route. Talk to people, find out their money spends, their habits, anything that would bring in new custom, should you set up in their area. Assess not only the possible volume of sales, but your customer type.

Also if you are not the first franchisee for the company, then make sure to visit, observe, and talk, to those running the other outlets to discover how their business is doing, and if they are happy with the relationship with the franchisor. More often than not, they will be more than willing to share their experiences with you, once you can establish some credibility and trust with them.

A franchise is an attractive option, but it can be expensive, particularly if you do not get sufficient sales revenue to sustain the high costs involved and to meet the requirements of the terms of your agreement. Always read the small print carefully. Always negotiate on any clauses that you are unhappy with in the contract. It is also important to also ensure that an opt-out clause exists in the contract, and, if it does not exist, then ensure that it is written into it, as often the penalties for breaking a franchise contract are high. So embrace your own power. Negotiate.

Remember that the business that becomes a franchise started out as a small business. Turning your business into a franchise is an option that perhaps more businesses, once established, should consider, as it helps to grow the brand name, as well as increase revenue. It also allows others to grow your success and become part of it.

So be patient. Believe in your vision, and at the same time, be awake to consumer needs and opportunities in the market place, at home and abroad.

When a franchise may not be for you

If you are going into business to be independent, to use your own initiative, and do things your way, then this is not for you. If you have to borrow all the money for a franchise and do not feel passionate about working in that particular business, and playing by the franchisor's rules, then the franchise option is not for you!

When a franchise may be for you

If you wish to receive a limited amount of business training, direct instruction on how to conduct the business, training for your staff, specifics as to how the business must operate, then this is for you! Areas normally covered by the franchisor are: customer care, logos, all interior layout and the regular reporting formats. It also includes meeting for regular business operation reviews and revenue trends. A franchisor will normally offer ongoing advice and support to the franchisee as the contract normally stipulates that the franchisor receives a percentage of the profits, so it is of mutual benefit that the franchise business outlet is profitable, and seeks to grow year on year.

For information on established franchise opportunities in Ireland and abroad, the following website is an interesting visit
http://www.franchisedirect.co.uk/about/

Section 3

Intellectual property rights (IPRS)

Protecting your work

Intellectual property rights (IPRS), often referred to as IP for short, are the exclusive legal protection rights given by government offices to persons for the use of the products of their minds, in other words, creative work. Examples include: inventions, designs, ideas, music, video or audio recordings, broadcasts, poems, journalistic works, architectural drawings, and maps. These rights usually extend for a particular period of time. They allow the creator (originator) legal ownership of their creative works, and its use by any other party is illegal, unless formal permission is obtained. This permission is obtained in advance of use, and normally this includes a fee, negotiated with the creator, for the use of the work for a specified period of time.

The objective is to prevent exploitation. This is enabled by putting a legal structure in place that offers some facility to protect and compensate the creators of creative works. It is up to the registered owner of the IP to negotiate with the person or corporation that wishes to use or license their registered Intellectual Property (rights to the creative work). Guidelines for minimum rates to the creators, in the negotiation with potential users, are often set down by professional bodies within the respective disciplines, for example, by the National Union of Journalists (NUJ) for journalistic writings.

There are occasions when it is best to talk to professionals who are accustomed to negotiation. An example might be, book rights being secured for film rights. In this case it would be best to go to a literary agent who specializes in this area, who would be accustomed to negotiating big contracts with film producers/studios. There are also agents available for many different business sectors. Other useful contacts are, your local or national intellectual property rights registration office (normally a Government Office), or your local/national Enterprise Board, or, alternatively, visit the website of the World Intellectual Property Organization[1]. IPRS are territorial. This means they only provide protection in the countries in which the intellectual property is registered. Unprotected products can be traded freely. Protected items being traded or seen in unprotected countries means that they can be copied without any recourse by the owner of the item in that country.

National and international laws and conventions are responsible for the recognition of the person's mental efforts as an intellectual property right. The World Intellectual Property Organization website gives information on the history of its formation, which makes an interesting read. In some cases of intellectual property rights, countries are signed up to conventions and are part of international alliances where particular IPs are recognized across the territories of the member countries.

The most common types of intellectual property rights (IPRS) are:-

   i.   Copyright
   ii.   Re-sale rights for artists
   iii. Designs
   iv.   Patents
   v.   Trade Marks

i.   Copyright

This protects material such as literature, art, music, sound recordings, films and broadcasts. Copyright became an international IP with the formation of the Berne Convention for the Protection of Literary and Artistic Works. It offers nationals protection for their creative works on an international platform, and facilitates the payment to the registered owners of the creative work. Such works include multimedia films, maps, charts, plans, software, radio and television broadcasts, drawings, paintings, sculptures, architectural works, songs,

---

1   www.wipo.int/

music (songs, operas, musicals, sonatas etc), plus novels, short stories, poems, and plays.

ii.   Re-sale rights for artists

Re-Sale Rights for Artists is a relatively new intellectual property right, introduced into both Ireland (June 2006) and the United Kingdom (February 2006). It is a result of a European Union Directive on the Resale Rights of Authors of Original Works of Art. This law entitles the creators of artwork, from within the European Economic Area[1] (EEA), to claim a royalty in the event of a resale, within certain terms and conditions. There are approximately 40 collecting societies for artists across the globe.

In Ireland the royalties are collected and distributed by the Irish Visual Artists Rights Organization[2] (IVARO) on behalf of its members. Irish Visual Artists Rights Organization is a not-for-profit organization, created to protect the copyright and related rights of artists and visual creators in Ireland and worldwide. In the UK the most prominent agency responsible for managing the resale rights on behalf of artists is the Design and Artists Copyright Society[3] (DACS). It is also a not-for-profit organization. DACS promotes and protects the copyright for artists and visual creators in the UK and worldwide. Members include architects, designers, craftspeople, printmakers, illustrators, photographers, sculptors and painters. Through a partnership with 32 agents in 27 countries, DACS offers representation to international artists as well as UK artists, and provides a global licensing service, and can be approached by either artists or clients (client being a person or organization wishing to obtain a license to use the work/s of a DACS member).

iii.   Designs

The appearance of a product - its features, such as shape, configuration, contours, texture, or materials of the product itself (not dictated by functional considerations) - is the result of its design, and can represent the whole or part of it. In summary, intellectual property rights for designs protect the visual appearance and/or eye appeal of products.

iv.   Trade marks

Brand identity is associated with trade marks, which can be distinctive words, name, symbols, or other features. Trade marks allow for differentiation between

1   http://ec.europa.eu/external_relations/eea/
2   http://www.ivaro.ie
3   http://www.dacs.org.uk/

traders, products and services and this IP protects the registered identification characteristic/s for the owner/s.

v.   Patents

A patent becomes an intellectual property right when a government agency (Patent and Trade Marks Office) issues a declaration recognizing a person or persons as the inventor of a new invention. This gives the declared inventor the privilege of stopping others from making, using, or selling, the claimed invention. Products can be new and/or improved. Also processes, and/or uses capable of industrial application, can also be registered as a patent.

Comment: Patents tend to be very expensive. They are also detailed and technical, and can become out of date if you change a little detail of what you have already registered. Investigate all options and then decide on your best course of action. Perhaps you might consider seeking a strategic partner who would take care of some of the major costs involved in registering a patent. If you endeavour to do it all yourself, then you may find that the patent gobbles up all your money, leaving little to none for the running of your business.

Section 4

How to register as self-employed

Introduction

Setting up a business can be challenging due, sometimes, to a lack of information on the processes and registrations required. But once you have decided on your business identity, be it a sole trader, company, partnership, charity, or cooperative, then the decisions on what needs to be done become clearer.

The Office of the Revenue Commissioners was established in the Republic of Ireland by Government Order in 1923, and its core business is the assessment and collection of taxes and duties. The Revenue Commissioners Office also provides information and services online through their website: http://www.revenue.ie It has two main taxation systems for the processing of income tax due (including capital gains tax), and they are:-

(a) Pay As You Earn (PAYE)
This applies to those in employment - they are taxed at source by their employer

(b) Pay and File, Self-Assessment System
This applies to those working for themselves - they are responsible for submitting their own tax documentation (returns) and payments. This applies to sole traders, companies, partnerships and trusts. When you are starting up a business/becoming self-employed, you are legally obliged to advise the Revenue Office, and this process is completed by registering your self-employment taxation status.

Steps to self-employment status

Below is an overview of what you are required to do to register as self-employed and operate within the law. You are:-

i.   legally required to register a business name, if you are setting up a sole trader business within the republic of Ireland, when the name is not your own name. This generally includes any online business operation, particularly a .ie business.

ii.   legally obliged to complete the appropriate Revenue forms to register for Self-Assessment tax, and submit your income tax returns, payable each year by 31 October, through the Pay and File facility.

iii.   legally obliged to register as an employer if you intend to employ workers as you are legally required to pay the employer's percentage of each worker's PRSI and pension contribution

iv.   legally obliged as a self-employed person to pay your Pay Related Social Insurance (PRSI)

v.   legally obliged to register for VAT in specific cases (details in VAT section)

Note: Insurance is obligatory in some situations, but every self-employed person would be advised to check out their individual and business needs, particularly in the area of public liability/third party fire and theft, and professional indemnity.

Registration of a business name

If you - as an individual, sole trader, part of a partnership or body corporate – intend to carry on a business under a name which is not wholly your own, then you are required to register a business name. A business name offers no legal protection. It is merely a means to being able to record the owners of businesses/business names. To register a business name in Ireland, a form must be completed and a small fee must be paid, which can be done online or by post to the Company's Registration Office.
Website: http://www.cro.ie

Registering for self-employment (taxation)

If you are setting up as self-employed, a sole trader, trust or partnership, then you need to complete and submit a Registration Form (TR1), which can be obtained from your local Revenue Office, within your Revenue District. The form can also be downloaded, completed and submitted online, on the Revenue website. If you intend to become an employer, then you will need to complete a PREM Registration Form for Employers (PAYE/PRSI) Tax Registration Form. Either of these two forms can also be used to register for income tax, employer's PAYE/PRSI, VAT, and relevant contracts tax. If you are setting up as a company, then you would only need to complete and submit a Registration Form for Companies (TR2). This form can also be used to register for corporation tax, VAT, and relevant contracts tax.

The tax year

The tax year begins on 1st January and ends on 31 December, but tax returns must be submitted at an earlier date. Pay and File is the term applied to the payment of tax and filing (lodging) of returns, and a single date is provided for this, normally 31 October.

Preliminary tax

The tax due concerns an estimate of income tax due for the current year (often referred to as preliminary tax), as well as any balance of tax due from the previous year. As a start-up business, you will not be charged interest on unpaid

preliminary tax in your start-up year, but it is best practice to pay the estimated tax due as close to your liability date as possible (31 October, your pay and file date), as this will help you to avoid cash flow stress when the total amount becomes due in the following year. The taxation classes catered for in the self-assessment tax return system are both income tax, and capital gains tax.

Income tax

This is paid on income earned in the tax year. As an employee, it is deducted from your earnings at source by your employer under the PAYE system. As a self-employed person, you are legally responsible for paying your own tax, which is paid through the self-assessment system. If you are late submitting your tax, penalties normally apply. The estimated income tax, referred to as preliminary tax, also includes RSI and health contributions. Normally (i.e. if not in your start-up year), to avoid paying interest penalties on your preliminary tax – it is the lower of 90% of our final liability to tax for the current tax year, or 100% of your liability to tax for the immediate previous year. A different condition applies if you pay your tax by direct debit and/or if your tax payable in the previous year is nil. The Revenue Office has endeavoured to make it easier for businesses to pay their taxes through a preliminary tax by direct debit scheme. Your local revenue office can assist you with queries.
Website: http://www.revenue.ie

RSI

This is an acronym for Pay Related Social Insurance, which the self-employed are legally obliged to pay to the state, as are employees and employers. The rate charged is a percentage of wages after pension contributions. It represents a contribution to both social insurance and the health service.

Capital gains tax

This tax refers to tax due on the disposal (sale) of assets, such as shares, buildings, machines, etc. This tax is payable in either of two periods, depending upon when the asset was disposed of or sold. The 'initial period' (1 January to 30 September, which must be paid before the end of the following month, i.e. 31 October (the pay and file date), and the later period, 1st October to 31 December, must be paid by the end of the following month, i.e. January 31. As relief will be due on most assets, such as depreciation, you would be well advised to seek the assistance of an accountant prior to making your capital gains tax return.

Related contracts tax

This tax concerns payments made by principle contractors operating in the field of construction, forestry or meat processing, who contract out or supply labour for the performance of relevant operations.

Tax credits

Tax credits were introduced in 2001 and replaced the tax free allowance system used by the Revenue Office. Some tax credits are awarded by the Revenue Office (the equivalent of the tax free allowance) and some must be applied for directly by the person and/or business. In the event of a refund of tax being due, it is carried over to the following year as a tax credit. Tax credits are issued for a percentage of the total paid to, for example, pension contributions, medical insurance contributions, union fees, education fees, dental bills, etc. Also, if self-employed, you can get tax credits for a percentage of the costs incurred in running your business, for example, rent on premises, and some travel and meeting expenses.

Double-income processing

If you have a PAYE job and also operate a small low-income business, you need not necessarily register as self-employed. You can pay the income tax due from your business activities separately and can arrange to have the tax due deducted under the PAYE system by reducing your tax credits and standard rate cut-off point. So one tax return only should be submitted. If you find yourself in this situation, it is best to seek advice from your own Revenue District Office.

Tax clearance certification

This is a written confirmation, issued on request to an individual or business, stating that their tax affairs are in order at date of issue of the certificate. The tax clearance certificate exists to ensure that government contracts (state money), grants and state licenses are only given to tax complaint bodies and individuals. Should you wish to request a tax clearance certification, visit the online services section of the Revenue website: www.revenue.ie/ or contact your local Revenue Office for details.

Value added tax (VAT)

Anyone carrying on a business (engaged in trading goods or services) is required by law to register for VAT[1], once their turnover exceeds a threshold defined by the government. This currently stands at 35,000 euro for services and 70,000 euro for goods. However, those with a turnover of less than this threshold can choose to register for VAT. Goods and services traded are inclusive of imported goods or services traded within the state, be they imported from within or outside of the European Union member countries.

Registering for VAT allows the trader to obtain a tax credit on their VAT outputs (paid) against their VAT liability (due to be paid). All transactions must be documented through correct VAT listing on invoices. For the process to work, all invoices received and given must have the trader's VAT registered number quoted on them, and must be retained for inspection by the Revenue Commissioner, if/when required as evidence of correct process having been transacted.

VAT is not deductible for reclaim purposes on a number of areas, such as the purchase of food, drink, accommodation or entertainment expenses for the trader, his staff or family, nor can it be deducted on petrol expenses if not stock in trade. The current standard rate of VAT is 21%. However, there are a few categories for which lower rates apply and defined areas which are VAT exempt. If you are unsure of a rate, double-check on the revenue website.

To register for VAT as either an individual or company, a form must be completed and submitted to your local revenue district. All details in relation to

---

1   http://www.taxireland.ie/taxadvice/ValueAddedTax.aspx

VAT rates and registration within the Republic of Ireland are available on the Irish Government's Revenue website: www.revenue.ie/tax/vat The European Union issues VAT Directives to member states, who must then modify their VAT legislation accordingly. In the event of any inconsistency, EU Law takes precedence over Irish legislation.

Recommendation

It is recommended that you visit the Revenue website, which provides a vast amount of detailed information of relevance to the self-employed, and the PAYE worker. This is only a guide to help you to establish perspective in what is required of you as a start-up. There are over 1,000 Irish Government offices nationwide.
Website: http://www.revenue.ie

Section 5

The employment of staff and contract workers

Introduction

When you start out in business, you will never be certain of how the business will progress, and in exactly what direction, as opportunities arise and you may decide to run with some of them. Despite having a detailed business plan, you can never be guaranteed of the extent of expertise that you will need, the amount of time that it will take to complete tasks, nor your own capacity to do everything!

So you need to be aware of the different types of employment terms available, the legal obligations, and worker rights which exist. As an entrepreneur, you will be concerned with finding the best candidate to perform the work that you need completed, and finding the best employment terms to suit your budget and business needs, and, at the same time, you must ensure that you are compliant with the law.

Flexible working

Flexibility was becoming common in the work place, prior to the arrival of the reduced economic activity across well established sectors. Now it is perhaps going to become a standard way of working in the coming decades. Perhaps it was a result of the boom years, teamed with a string of other developments in the current ways of working. Other factors include, changes in people's lifestyles such as two working parents; increased worker rights due to new labour-related legislation (the result of directives) which are enforced at national level by the European Union (EU); the greater availability of workers from some European-Union countries and from Asia; the introduction of minimum wage legislation; the increase in education levels; and the fast dissemination of information due to widespread availability of the internet. Flexible working arrangements include:-

i.   Fixed-term
ii. Part-time
iii. Casual
iv. Temporary agency working

i.   Fixed term worker

This type of worker contract has a specific start and finish date, and is often engaged to perform a specific task or project. Also, the period of contract may be extended, dependant upon certain criteria, for example, securing additional commission or additional funding being made available from an external source. However, according to the Protection of Employees (Fixed-Term Work) Act,2003, there are criteria in place which stipulate that employees cannot remain on fixed-term contracts indefinitely. If you are employing a person for the first time since July 2003, (the date the above law was enacted), then the combined duration of the contracts shall not exceed four years. After this, if the employer wishes the employee to continue, it must be with a contract of indefinite duration.

ii. Part-time worker

A part-time employee is someone who works less hours than a comparable full-time employee doing the same type of work. The Protection of Employees (Part-Time Work) Act, 2001 states that workers engaged in part-time work must not be treated any less favourably in employment conditions than those in fixed-term or indefinite contracts.

iii. Casual worker

This term applies to an individual who works for a period of less than thirteen continuous weeks, and the work performed by this individual is not regarded as being seasonal or regular employment.

iv. Temporary agency worker

This is where the employer asks an appropriate employment agency to provide a worker, with the required skills, to perform specified work for a specified period of time. The Temporary Agency Worker is employed by the Agency and contracted out to the third party, for example, your business. Your contract is with the Employment Agency. This type of worker is also entitled to the same conditions of employment as fixed-term contract workers.

The employer's obligation

If you employ a person, then you are obliged, by a legal duty of care, to ensure that your worker receives all their due employment rights. These worker rights are enabled by labour laws and associated legislation. It is in your own interest, and can save you long-term, if you maintain employee details, such as: name, address, RSI number, the hours they work, breaks, annual leave, and other employment-related entitlements, so that you will be able to prove that you are compliant with employment rights legislation, should the need arise.

Below is a list of the basic worker rights, which will be helpful to you when you are nearing the time to consider taking on someone to assist you in your business:-

- Within a period of two months of starting work, under the Terms of Employment (Information) Act 1994, and 2001, the employer must issue in writing to the employee, the terms and conditions of the worker's employment. This includes details in regards to title and nature of their work, sick pay, cessation of employment (if a fixed term employee), how their pay is calculated, and the duration of employment and/or in what situations their employment will cease.

- A payslip must be issued in written form, outlining the gross and net wage and all deductions made.

- The minimum wage must be met, which, for an experienced adult working in the Republic of Ireland, was €8.65 per hour in June 2010. Variations exist, and are mainly: if the person is a close relative, if the worker is a trainee, and/or if they are under 18 years of age. Also, exceptions apply to particular industries. See: website: www.nera.ie/someindustries.

- The maximum working week allowed is 48 hours, and this can be calculated over a four, six or twelve month period, depending on the industry. Employers must keep a record of the number of hours the employee works.

- A worker has the right to take a 15 minute break, if working continuously for four and a half hours, and is entitled to a 30 minute break after working continuously for six hours. These are unpaid breaks.

- The cessation of employment has to be carefully managed, as there are procedures to be followed, be they for example, a dismissal, or the ending of employment by one or both parties (i.e. employee and employer). A minimum amount of notice must be given to the worker on the termination of their employment - the statutory minimum duration depends upon the number of years they have been working with your business.

Sources of information

You only need to know the information that relates to your needs and those of your business. However, labour-related information is widely available - from government, private and industry-related organisations, and many provide direct customer services and/or websites. Among the most reliable examples are:-

The National Employment Rights Authority (NERA) provides information on employment legislation and related rights for both the employer and the employee.
NERA: http://www.employmentrights.ie/en/

Also, if you wish to investigate the same employment legislation and rights from a worker's perspective, the Services, Industrial, Professional and Technical Union (SIPTU) provides both support and information.
SIPTU: http://www.siptu.ie/

Although online networking sites and forums cannot be relied upon in a legal dispute, they can be most helpful in giving you a point in the right direction, if you have queries. However, details of employee issues should always be kept confidential. So, if posing a question, keep it general, as the internet is an open forum and you should protect the reputation and confidentiality of how you conduct your business. An example of a forum is:
http://www.Boards.ie

Another useful service worth investigating is:
http://www.EmployerAdvice.ie

Section 6

Why take out professional indemnity insurance

Professional indemnity insurance protects business interests against claims for professional neglect, as well as errors and omissions, for both the principles and their employees. Professional indemnity insurance may also be referred to as professional negligence insurance, or errors and omissions insurance.

There is normally a duty of care requiring the worker to show reasonable care and skill in the performance of any task assigned and/or undertaken in a professional capacity. If the person is negligent (not showing a duty of care), they can be made liable for any losses incurred, injury or damage caused. This normally results in a court case in order to prove negligence and recoup the losses – through the replacement of goods, compensation for the perceived injury or damage. Professional Indemnity protects the professional who carries out the work.

This is an important insurance consideration for anyone contracting out their services and/or who, as part of a business, promotes and manages the services of other professionals. Also, if you employ staff, then you will have them engaged in contract of service, i.e. they will receive all the benefits and protection under employment legislation, and, ultimately, you as the employer are responsible for the activities carried out by your business. Professional Insurance is compulsory for some professions, for example, architects, solicitors, accountants, financial advisers, and consultants.

As a professional, and an entrepreneur, you do need to protect against being sued. You need to protect your reputation, and that of your business, in the event of a client being unhappy with a service and/or product, by being able to offer compensation. To assess your needs you need to, firstly, consider your proposed business activities for the next year, (one year at a time). Secondly, I suggest that you talk to different insurance brokers to get feedback on their perception of your professional indemnity needs, get quotes, and then draw your own conclusions as to your level of professional insurance need. This could be the best investment that you ever made, for your long-term business success and your own peace of mind.

General Insurance Information

The Irish Insurance Federation (IIF) runs a free Insurance Information Service (IIS) for members of the public. The contact details are: phone: 01-6761914; fax: 01-6761943; email: iis@iif.ie A query form is also available on their website, which can be completed and submitted online, website: http://www.iif.ie/iis

PART 8

FINANCE AND ACCOUNTING

Section 1
- Introduction

- Background

- Sources of finance

- Tracking your transactions

- The language of business – accounting

- Summary-why bother with accounting

Section 2
- The accounting process – the two-stop jargon journey

- The balanced scorecard

- Avoid bad debts/cash collection tips

- Registering for taxation/VAT

- Bibi's choice

Finance and Accounting

Section 1

Introduction

In this section we take a look at two major areas, finance and accounting. Finance, as the term implies, is concerned with the sourcing of the funds for the operation and activities of the business, and investing opportunities. Accounting is the systematic recording, reporting and analysis of financial transactions of a business. It varies in detail between countries and some industry sectors. It presents both administrative and management perspectives, that help the owner/manager to make better judgements and decisions concerning the business.

Background

It has been normal practice, up to mid-2009, for most businesses to rely on financial facilities, such as loans and overdrafts from banks and other financial institutions to meet their bills during low cash flow periods and/or to sustain their existence during times of low-profit. When the banks began to greatly reduce their finance facilities to businesses, this meant that some loans were not renewed, others were recalled at short notice, and some had their financial facilities reduced or stopped. This resulted in hundreds of small and medium sized businesses simply being forced to downsize dramatically, and some were forced to close.

Now this is the backdrop against which you are going to set up a business in the coming two to perhaps five years. So you know that whatever you decide to do, your business must be sustainable, as in the short-term it will have less financial support compared to other young businesses started during the old system. The same financial doors may not be open to you, but innovative thinking and technology should be among your greatest assets, and as the saying goes:

when one door closes another one opens

Sources of finance

Some Credit Unions are beginning to formally open their doors to the business community. With reduced services available from most banks, other organisations, which have been in existence for a long time, will now be relied upon even more, as a source of finance. Some of these also offer mentoring and training for budding and developing entrepreneurs. These include Local Authorities, The Enterprise Boards, Enterprise Ireland, the Industrial Development Authority (IDA), Inter-Trade Ireland, and other enterprise and industry-supporting organisations. Big industry companies and some Universities are always keen to sponsor research and development, and become involved in start-up businesses in the areas of science and technology. The Arts Council and Visual Arts Ireland provide some funding for creative-focused initiatives.
(Some finance resources will be listed at a later stage on the following website: http://www.peel-your-own-orange.ie)

Tracking your transactions

It is important that you open a separate bank account for your business. Basic as it may sound, it is necessary to keep your business transactions separate from your personal finances. This avoids confusion at a later date when you try to track your spending and general financial activity. When it comes to opening an account, the bank/financial institution will require certain information and documentation. These include proof of your name along with photo identity verification, proof of your home and/or business address, and your signature. You will also be required to give the names and signatures of those who will have access to the business account.

It is between you and the bank to agree on the type of account, cheque book, pin and chip or both, the overdraft limit, the foreign bank transaction facility, and any other facilities required. A lot is dependent upon business needs and your own history with the bank. Bank policy and support initiatives operated by the bank/financial institution will influence your success in obtaining all that you seek from them.

The language of business - accounting

Accounting is the language of business. From accounts, one can get an over-view of the business, rather like a satellite view! As a result, you can see at a glance, for example, what the sales are, how much bank savings the business has accumulated, what the loan repayments are, and what the overheads cost. Accounts give a bird's-eye-view of the activity level and financial state of the business at a particular point in time. Accounting transactions are normally put into categories so that it is easy to compare figures year on year and also easy to extract information quickly, no matter who is viewing your books. By compar-ing years, having used the same terms for the various expenses in the business, (for example, transport, cash, sundries etc), one can compare expenses across years and note trends, such as increasing transport costs, decreasing wages and bank repayments, or cash in the bank increasing.

Most people preparing to start-up a business wish to ignore the book-keeping and accounts aspect of it. However, it is the tracking of transactions that will give you confidence as you come to understand the key management functions required to reduce risk, and continue to step forward, maintaining and develop-ing your business. Budgeting, which we covered in Part 3 of this book, will help you to plan and control your spending, as it allocates resources to different areas based on the amount of money that you have to spend. Accounting records what you have done, but also helps you to plan, by comparing trends to previous accounting periods. By planning your spending you can control it. For example, if you decide on the cost of your next contract or job, or the value of the goods that you need to purchase for resale, then you can plan at how much you need to sell your next contract or job in order to meet your cash spend requirement. It is your business. It is your responsibility. You have to manage your finances, and that means keeping a close eye on all of your transactions and planned spends.

In most cases, a business will see their accountant maybe once or twice a year. The accountant endeavours to do the small business's books as quickly as pos-sible, to get paid, and to keep you happy enough to keep you on his books as a paying customer. That is his business. Time is money. It is up to you to pay close attention to the affairs of your business, however, an accountant may offer you advice, but nobody knows your business like you do! This book considers that you have little or no knowledge of the accounting processes. It gives a fee' for the terminology and opens you up to the thought processes involved. A mentioned earlier, a comprehensive analysis of accounting is beyond the sco; it is a book or even a series of books all in itself!

However, some of you may have experienced some level of book-keeping or business studies. Some of you may have done so at third level. Others may have taken courses that excluded any business training or insights. Whatever the case, the fact remains that you will need some level of knowledge in this area to build and manage your own business successfully. It is important, also, to show that you understand this area when it comes to doing business with a bank manager, your grant provider, a potential investor, a sponsor or your accountant. Whatever the many reasons, your knowledge will give you greater confidence to deal with any business and personal situation, and will also inspire confidence in you from people doing business with you.

Although there are now many computerised financial packages available, you still need to understand the basic book-keeping and accounting principles in order to make any sense of what you are doing. So no matter what legal entity you set up – sole trader, limited company, partnership or other – you will need to be able to work with the accountant when he gets to review your books prior to submitting your final figures to the Revenue Office at the end of the financial year. Some creative sectors are exempt from tax in some countries (Ireland, for example); however, you will still be required to submit your figures to the Revenue Office.

To interpret financial information for your own business needs, you need to know what to look for, and what information you need to source, track and forecast. If you are past the start-up phase, then look at past transactions, (historical information), in order to get some picture of your future resource needs. Historical information, combined with market trends, is used by most businesses to forecast the costs and other resources required for the coming year. These forecasts are normally termed 'projections'.

If you are in start-up phase, you can find case studies on the internet, and carry out continuous market research, yourself, in order to predict your needs in response to estimated consumer demand. Of course, there will be an element of risk involved. The general warning is that you normally need more money to run your business than you expect, but you must believe that you will always find a way to meet your needs. So navigate positively around your challenges as they arise.

Summary - why bother with accounting?

- it records business transactions
- it helps track trends across periods of time, such as trends in sales, profit, purchases, and can show how busy your business was, or not, during any given time span
- it shows the profit or loss you make, and accounts can often help to answer why
- it allows you share your information easily with other people, for example, if you wish to bring an investor into your business, such as a business partner; a partner will need a clear picture of the history of your business before investing
- it shows the financial and sales situation of your business at a given time; the accounts can be used to support your application for grants or loans, if you have reached that stage
- it helps you to plan where your business is going and how it is going to get there (business strategy)
- it allows you to compare performances – actual with what you had intended. It allows you to then decide on the corrective action where, when and if necessary
- if you are a company, you are legally required to maintain accounts and have them signed off by an accountant and submit them annually to the Company's Registration Office (http://www.cro.ie)
- if you are a sole trader, you are still required to keep accounts and submit them for review by the tax office in support of your assessment of your tax liability.

Section 2

The accounting process - the two-stop jargon journey

Introduction

The journey of financial transactions, from start-up costs to the day-to-day business transactions, including discounts and tax, are all tracked through the two-stop accounting process. This is a journey for which you are fully responsible. The transactions begin in the books of first entry and end up in the boc s

of final accounts. It is important to reiterate that this is just a snap-shot of the accounting process, as accountants spend years developing this expertise. The aim of this section is to introduce accounting terminology and give you an overview of how the process works.

STOP 1: The books of first entry

First stop on the accounting journey is the books of first entry, where business transactions are recorded for the first time. The key books of first entry are:-

   i.   The sales book
   ii. The sales returns book
   iii. The purchases book
   iv. The purchases return book
   v. The cash book.

i.   The sales book

Sales records can be maintained easily in the sales book, which is a straight forward list of all sales made in a particular period of time.

Credit sales are goods for resale in a business and are normally given 28 days within which time payment must be made for the goods.

ii.   Sales returns book

The value and description of the goods returned to your business by customers are entered into this book.

iii. The purchases book

Goods or services bought on credit (on account) for the purpose of sale are entered in the purchases book.

iv. The purchase returns journal

The value and description of the goods returned by your business to the supplier from whom they were bought are entered into this book.

v.   The cash book

A book used to record details of cash moving in and out of the business current account. As a control check, it is good practice to compare the cash balance in the cash book to the balance on the business bank statement, to ensure that they are the same, and, if not, the you need to identify the reasons for any differences by comparing details.

The ledger accounts

Ledgers record summarized information originally recorded in the books of first entry (Stop 1). The ledgers sit between the book of first entry and the final accounts, and are also called the books of final entry.

The ledgers consist of the general ledger and subsidiary ledgers. The general ledger summarises all of the company's financial transactions and contain a series of accounts for all aspects of the business – revenue, expenses, assets etc.

In advance of preparing accounts (Stop 2), a list of all the accounts is printed. This is called the trial balance, and shows the opening and closing balance on each account. Some accounts have a debit balance and others have a credit balance. These balances equal each other i.e. the sum of the debits equals the sum of the credits. That is why you often hear the term 'balance the books'.

While accounting may seem straightforward, it is a staged process, which you will learn to understand fairly quickly.

Only the totals from the books of first entry are brought forward to the trial balance accounting process, which is regarded as a check and balance system. This ensures that you have recorded your transactions correctly.

It is a staged process. If all the entries were put into just one book, it would not be easy to find or extract information or to read at a glance your state of business affairs at any given time. It is from the trial balance that the totals are taken to the books of final accounts.

STOP 2: The books of final accounts

This is the second and last main stop on the accounting journey, the books of final accounts, consisting of three main books of major significance to any business. They are:-

   i.   the cash flow statement
   ii. the profit and loss account
   iii. the balance sheet

i.   The cash flow statement (CFS)

The CFS is very important for you in order to help you to budget for your incoming bills, such as loan repayments, electricity, gas, telephone, broadband,

A very simple overview of the cash flow process is:
Cash in less cash out = Cash in hand.

ii.   The profit & loss account

This records all the income and expenditure incurred in the running of the business during the year, and from these you can extract the gross, and then the net profit (or loss) of a business.

Gross profit (or loss): sales less cost of the sales of your product or service.

Net profit (or loss): gross profit (or loss) less all other operating costs for the business (payroll, tax, light, heat, electricity, etc)

Example

Sales		50,000	
Less cost of sales			
Purchases	10,000		
Marketing	2,000	12,000	
Gross Profit			**38,000**
Less expenses			
Salaries	5,000		
Light/heat	2,000		
Rent	3,000		
Packaging	200		
Transport	1,000	11,200	
Net Profit			**26,800**

iii.   The balance sheet

It can be regarded as the window into the financial position of the business/organisation. It shows what the business owns in the listing under assets, (such as cash in bank, finished products, motor vehicles, premises, stock) and owes, listed under liabilities, (bank borrowings, capital owed to investors). It would normally be written up once a month.

these books of final a count th iness manager (probably you) can
nformation to produ e wha d as management
ared monthly to pr

you make decisions. These management accounts are aimed at internal users of the information. Figures can be analysed to find evidence of trends in the company's operations and markets. They can compare year on year accounts. Financial accounts, aimed at external users of financial information, will have to be prepared annually. These concentrate on the business as a whole and contain less detailed information than management accounts. While many similarities apply between the two, financial accounts are focused on an external audience and, unlike the management accounts, are not seen as an aid to decision making.

The balanced scorecard

The balance scorecard was developed to guide businesses to look beyond financial performance (profit trends) as the sole indicator of success. The thinking behind it was that financial performance was based on the past and was not necessarily an indicator of future success. The first balanced scorecard was created in 1987 by Art Schneiderman (an independent consultant on the management of processes) at Analog Devices.[1]

The aim was to focus on what managers are doing now to create future value for their business and owners. It is regarded as a means of creating value through sustained performance improvement. The balanced scorecard was developed to assist big companies. It was not aimed at start-ups, which have no history, but it has significance for anyone with an interest in business start-up and development. However, I really want you to be aware of its existence, as you might decide to keep it in mind and perhaps personalise it for your own business, now and as you progress.

Measuring performance

The framework of the balanced scorecard introduces four areas where a business should, and can, measure its performance, and these are generally considered to be predictive of future business success. The four categories are:-

   i.   Financial
  ii.   Customer
 iii.   Process
 iv.   Learning/growth

i.   financial

An example of the financial perspective might be to ensure that the accounting system reflects the financial needs of the business accurately at any given time, that costs and business plans are reviewed regularly, and possibilities for progress are sought, and that management accounts can be produced easily.

ii.   customer

An example of customer orientation could be ensuring that the ordering system is modern and efficient and/or developing a better customer feedback system

iii.   process

The internal process perspective might be improving the ordering system, the development of a more efficient tracking and delivery service, better quality assessment, and obtaining quality mark standards, where possible.

iv.   learning and growth

This could be setting the objective of retaining top skilled workers, predicting future innovations, giving final year or graduate students opportunities to introduce innovative ideas in select parts of your business, or adopting innovation when it can increase your differentiation and competitive edge.

It is recommended that the business sets down three to five performance measures for each of the four dimensions (above), and these guide the business to achieve its long-term success. Developing a Balanced Scorecard guides a business to maintain a forward looking and progressive attitude, and to develop and be innovative in its operations in these key areas.

Avoid bad debts/cash collection tips

Be smart from the start and stay in business! When you are starting out in business you are keen to build relationships. However, you are also a potential target for exploiters of goodwill. So beware and be aware! My advice to you on giving extended credit is simply, don't! The lesson here is not to allow customer debts (debtors), and if you really need to give a little slack, do not allow the debt to sit or accumulate over a long period of time. Small businesses cannot afford to have debtors owing large or even small amounts of money for any periods of time.

Cash flow is the core need of every small to medium size business. It is what you have to monitor carefully every day. It is best to have a policy of 'no credit'. If that is impossible or unfavourable to you (and some clients), then establish a clear policy. Firstly, decide if the customer is suitable for credit. Are they likely to repay? While you are unlikely to carry out a formal credit check, it would be wise to ask around, speak to other companies dealing with the customer. If it is a substantial credit, then perhaps you could casually find out the name of the bank with which they do business. There is no harm in a phone call of enquiry, if you feel that they are a high risk.

Make sure that all your clients - current and potential - are aware of your credit policy. Create a notice stating that accounts must be cleared at the end of every calendar month (or 28 days), and display it in a prominent position in your place of business – store, on your website, and have it printed on your invoices and receipts.

If someone is slow to clear their account, then a phone call or reminder note may be required. Do not allow any further transactions on any outstanding account. Charging interest is fine, but if they do not pay in the end, then the interest is really being charged against yourself (your business). It takes time to manage debtor accounts (customer debts). That time, focus, and energy, would be better served being directed to your business activities, and looking for new business, or new revenue streams. Today, people have credit and debit cards, so make sure your business is set up to use both. So when it comes to avoiding bad debts, my advice is simple: be smart from the start and stay in business!

Tips for cash flow

Here are a few tips to help you to better manage your cash, as cash flow is the key factor that can choke an otherwise successful business.

- As discussed above, it is expensive to give credit to clients/customers, so it is best avoided.

- Ensure that you send your invoices to your clients promptly

- If you can get credit from another supplier that will give you interest for a period of about 28 days

- You can encourage clients to operate an annual budget account, where a customer pays an agreed amount say, 50 euro per month across the year, and they get a maximum credit of 600 euro (simply 50 x 12 months).

- Cheques received can be expensive, as it takes anything from three to five days to clear, when that money could be in your account.

- Accept credit card payments from clients as, although you will pay a fee to the credit card company, you get paid immediately, and it is then becomes the responsibility of the credit card company to get paid by the client.

- Paying cheques gives you a few days use of the money that will not be cleared from your account for at least three working days.

- Using a credit card to pay bills and then clearing it before interest becomes due, gives you cheap access to working capital. However, if you fail to pay before interest is charged, then it is an expensive charge on the use of the money. While there is a annual stamp duty on the cost of the card, normally 50 euro, which, over 12 months, is a small cost if you use the card wisely - by clearing the balance before interest becomes due.

- Be aware of the interest charged on your bank loan and/or overdraft as this is a direct cost to your business. Calculate how much it costs on a daily basis. When counting your profit, based on your business transactions for the day or week, i.e. after costs have been deducted, you must also take account of the cost of your credit facilities.

- Avoid having money tied up in stock if either will be waiting to be utilized for long spells of time.

- Avoid opting for high cost monthly payments on overheads, such as premises, motor vehicles, state-of-the-art machines, until your business and cash flow stabilises. However, considering that markets fluctuate and trends change, it is smart to keep overheads low enough so that your business is still attractive to clients/customers. Your core business must be the focus of your attention and receive cash to enable it to function. The trappings of your business must be secondary, if your business is to survive.

- Mobile phone usage is expensive. Where possible, try to use email or Skype for international calls, as this will reduce your cash outlay on phone bills. Also, check around with different mobile phone operators, as they are very competitive and good deals can be available.

- If possible pay bills late, unless there is a penalty for doing so, and so long as it does not affect your credit rating.

- If you operate your business on credit terms, ie 28 days, and if you are paying cash for your stock to supply your clients, be careful that you manage your sales across each month so that you do not run out of both cash and stock before your clients pay you. It would be best if you could offer some incentive to some clients to pay you cash on delivery (COD).

- If you are charging VAT, then you will need to make regular returns to the government Revenue Office. Ensure that you do not include the VAT charged to clients/customers as part of your revenue from sales, because when it comes to paying your VAT balance due to the government, you could find that it makes a big dip in the cash that you thought belonged to your business.

- If you plan to work with a client on an ongoing basis, you should negotiate a retainer, i.e. some money upfront and/or on a monthly basis. This client would normally get work done on credit, and when completed you would bill them. So you would need a retainer to maintain some cash flow in your business.

- It is advisable to arrange some sort of credit facility with a bank that you can activate if you find yourself running out of cash.

The above is to ignite your appreciation of the value of cash and how vital it is for the survival of your company to keep it both coming in, and in your possession for as long as possible. It is not so easy to manage your cash, particularly if you are a lone entrepreneur, always looking to the next sale, rather than ensuring that you get paid for the last contract/sale. So it would be good practice if you could get another person to assess, on a monthly basis, how you are managing your cash flow.

Registering for taxation

When it comes to registering for taxation, every trading company and self-employed person must register and file returns to the government's Revenue Department at the end of the financial year.

If you are a qualifying Artist in Ireland, then you may be income tax exempt on some/all of the revenue earned from your creative works. It is important to check out details on artist's exemptions, as it is open to change. However, you are still required to submit a tax return form declaring your income at year end to the Revenue Office. If you plan on employing staff you will need to sort out the tax contributions for your staff.

(For more on taxation/self-employment, the employment of staff, see Part 7)

Value added tax (VAT)

Anyone carrying on a business i.e. engaged in trading goods or services, is required by law to register for Value Added Tax (VAT), once their turnover exceeds a threshold defined by the government. This currently stands at 37,500 euro for services, and 75,000 euro for goods. However, those with a turnover of less than this threshold can choose to register for VAT.
http://www.taxireland.ie/taxadvice/ValueAddedTax.aspx

Some transactions are zero rated, depending upon the trading situation and the category of goods or services. It is best to seek advice from your local revenue office, verbally and in writing, prior to starting to trade, to ensure that you have the most up-to-date information. The European Union issues VAT Directives to member states, who must then modify their VAT legislation accordingly.

Registering for VAT allows the trader to obtain a tax credit on their VAT outputs (VAT paid) against their VAT liability (VAT due). All transactions must be documented through correct VAT listing on invoices. For the process to work, all invoices received   n must have the trader's VAT registered number quoted in th   ces ust also be retained for inspection by the R/ enue C mi   uired as evidence of correct process ha   een tr   cte

VAT is not deductible for reclaim purposes on a number of areas, such as the purchase of food, drink, accommodation, nor entertainment expenses for the trader, his staff or family; nor can it be deducted on petrol expenses if not stock in trade. The standard rate of VAT in June 2010 is 21%. However, there are some few categories for which lower and zero rates apply, and defined areas that are VAT exempt. VAT rates change from time to time, so check online now and again to ensure that you are up to date.

To register for VAT, as either an individual or business, a form must be completed and submitted to your local revenue district.

If you elect to register for VAT, you must charge on all your invoiced billings. You cannot opt for certain items as you choose. So think about whether you should register for VAT. Think about whether or not you should register a business name instead of your own name. All details in relation to VAT rates and registration within the Republic of Ireland are available on the Irish Government's Revenue website: www.revenue.ie/tax/vat
(For more on VAT, see Part 7)

Bibi's choice

A selection of business terms explained

Statement of Account: is a document, normally sent by the supplier, informing the person named on the document (addressee) of the current state of their account. It can show money due (a debit); or zero, if you have paid in full for your goods or services. If it shows a credit, then you have either overpaid or you have received a credit on your account, perhaps for returned goods, or a discount applied after the transaction for an unexpected reason, such as damaged goods or an overcharge refunded.

Bank Statement: is a similar document showing all the transactions on your account for the period outlined, including bank charges and the account balance at that end date. It is a good idea to review your bank balance to analyse your spending patterns, and be aware of the bank charges for the different transactions that you regularly use.

Creditor: A person or business to whom you owe money in return for goods or services.

Debtor: A person or business that owes you money in return for goods or services.

Bad Debt: If the person or business fails to honour their debt, then you may have to write it off as a bad debt. Prior to writing it off, you could send them a solicitor's letter, or, depending on the amount outstanding, you could take them to court, which is an expensive process, and also costly in terms of time taken away from focusing on your business. There are also businesses that make a business out of collecting debts, and that process is called factoring. By this method, you are paid a percentage of the debt by the factoring business, and the balance is written off in your books as a bad debt.

Liquidation: this term means to wind up a business. This normally happens when the company is unable to meet its debts, i.e. it is forced into liquidation. art o the process is the ap⁻ ᵐᵉnt of a liquidator, who oversees the selling ·ff of ᵉ assets nd sᵤ ' ᵣ c..dⁱ ᵤrs and debtors. It is part of the liquida- ᵣr's t ᵢk, also, ᵢ asᵣ ᵢᵢᵣ ᵢᵣ ᵗ' ᵣ ness parts can be sold off separately to ᵢingᵣ ᵣ ᵣ ᵣ ᵣ .d. ᵢᵦₜₛ.

Owners' Equity: the part of the net worth of the business due to the owner or owners of the business. It normally is the sum of the owners' investment in the business (shares) plus profit in the business which effectively belongs to the owners.

Book-Keeping: This is a system of recording monetary transactions of the business. Traditionally, this was a manually recorded system, but today it is done on computer, using specifically formulated accounts package software.

A Balance Sheet: this shows the financial position of a business at a given point in time, which is normally at year-end.

Turnover: the amount of money that the business is generating, and represents the total income of the business generated from sales and services within the accounting period.

Assets: (current, fixed, intangible and liquid): are resources of the business, and they have a monetary value that can be used in the future to provide benefits. For example: buildings, cash in bank and machinery/equipment used in the business. The main types of assets are: current assets, fixed assets, and intangible assets. Cash is a current asset, as it can easily be disposed of; buildings would be an example of a fixed asset as it is not so liquid (i.e. not so easily turned into cash). Intellectual property, such as a patent, is an example of an intangible asset. Examples of the most liquid assets are as follows: cash in bank, shares listed on the stock exchange and government bonds (the latter when normal economic conditions prevail). In summary, an asset is worth money to you.

A Liability: is a financial obligation on your business arising from a past transaction or event. Examples are: bank loans, creditors (people to whom you owe money), and long term leases payable.

Liquidity: This is a term used by financial specialists to describe the ability of a business to meet short-term financial obligations, in other words - can you pay your bills! Examples of such obligations are: bank loan repayments, payment for goods and services, wages to staff, lighting and heating bills, and other regular overhead costs that facilitate the day-to-day running of the business.

Embrace the person that you are

as you are the key to your success

You are your long-term advantage

through all seasons

Should you wish to register your feedback on this book, you would be most welcome.

email: **info@peel-your-own-orange.ie**

website: **www.peel-your-own-orange.ie**